BRILLIANCE

Understanding the Creative Mind

VOLUME I

Bennett Litwin & J. Schuh

First Edition, 2014

Printed in the United States of America

This labor of love is dedicated to artists of past generations who put their passion into the civilization we live in, and those who will build a better world through the changes you will effect on society.

Special thanks for their love and support, Rachel Schuh, Benjamin Schuh, Emily Schuh, Gayla Wilson, Adam Litwin, Ronda Litwin and a huge inspiration from Cameron Litwin.

Extra thank you for their friendship and assistance on this book, Ruth Litwin, Mark Gilpin, Brian Sullivan, Adam Litwin, A.J. Woods and Rick Villa.

We feel gratitude to Douglas King, our master chef, for putting the final design together on BRILLIANCE.

Finally, we remain humble and awed by the wonderful and inspiring authors whom we've studied and quoted as parts of this text.

Thank you, Dr. Carol Dweck, Richard Brodie, John Medina, David Rock, Mihaly Csikszentmihalyi, Tony Buzan, Barry Buzan, David Bayles, Ted Orland, Edward de Bono, Sam Harrison, The Dali Lama, Stefan Mumaw, Wendy Lee Oldfield, Doug Hall, and Roger von Oech.

Why did I write this book?

Well, the first answer is… Because my students asked me to. The second answer is… I didn't. Really, most of this book was written by my good friend and co-author, Bennett Litwin. I was just the guy who came up with the idea for the book, then handed over many books I'd read for reference and repeatedly said to him, "My students keep wanting me to write a book based on my lectures, and you're a writer, what do you think?" Luckily, he agreed. The book you are reading here is the product of thousands of hours of reading, research, and lunch meetings.

What are J's Lectures?

I have been doing what I call "Success Lectures" in all of my classes for over 10 years. Whether I was teaching Adobe After-Effects, Storyboarding or Animation, in every class my students got a lecture on information that I thought was important to being successful as a creative. Having run a thriving business doing animation, cartoons, design, and motion graphics for Fortune 500 companies, I've learned lessons about what is needed to be successful.

While teaching, I observed certain patterns over the years. First, I noticed that if I showed someone how to do something, but they didn't do it right away or at least when they got home, they tended to forget the information pretty quickly. The second thing I noticed was what prevents most students from doing good and even great work wasn't as much learning the fundamentals or how to use the tools in the software classes I taught. The real issue was the way they were thinking about the creative process and the time they spent on the projects.

"Fear" became a recurring emotion in my class. Let's face it, most people are at least nervous when they are learning something new; some are terrified. The more my students felt out of their comfort zone, the greater their fear became. One human reaction to fear is to procrastinate. I did the same thing while writing the very words you are reading here.

I don't consider myself a writer, and although I consider myself a good public speaker, my lectures always came from my heart in a very impromptu manner. Every lecture was different in some way. The basic information was the same, but the delivery was different every time. Saying it and writing it down are quite different.

I have shared with my students that the best way to overcome fear is to develop in yourself more desire than fear.

The greater the desire, the greater the odds are you will take action.

I have a great desire to not let down my students; especially the one's who have been waiting over ten years for this book to get done. So the lectures included in this book are my best efforts to do a montage of the lectures I have done in my classes over the years. To all my students who have waited so long for this book, I hope what I have written in my lectures lives up to your expectations. My lectures are placed throughout, in, and around the narrative, science, illustrations, quotes, psychology, and bios in BRILLIANCE. Enjoy it all.

INTRO TO BRILLIANCE

Everyone has a creative mind. Some people occasionally visit their creative place, while others live there. BRILLIANCE is constructed for those who live in their creative minds most of the time. For the rest, welcome to their world.

BRILLIANCE is for three groups of people:

1) Creative thinkers, artists

2) Humans who wish to better understand the artists in their lives

3) Humans who wish to develop their own creative thinking, and become more artistic

In the allegory that runs throughout the book, Mary is our protagonist. She's a few years out of high school, exploring junior college. Mary's perspective demonstrates how the creative mind is brilliant.

Mary's parents love her. Their feelings about her future range from freaked-out most days to almost okay on their good days. You see, Mary is an artist. Her parents are frightened about how the world will value Mary, and mostly, how she will make a living being so creative. They do not understand what motivates their daughter. Her life isn't logical.

Mary's school grades were all over the map. On occasion, Mary made excellent marks when she felt passion for the subject or love from the teacher.

Mary's life is directed by her heart, much more than by her intellect. She even excelled in one math class because she connected to the teacher. For Mary, it's about the people and the feelings, not the subject matter. How can she do so well in math one year and suck the next year? She didn't feel it the next year. It's that simple. Why don't her parents get it?

Mary's Blog

My Parents are Weird

September 1   3:05 pm

My first year of junior college started last week, and they're so worried that I'll hang out with other freaks like me or Goths or lesbians. Who do they think I'll sit with at lunch, the chess club? I'm taking pottery, which I'm totally psyched about, along with two required courses, a creative writing class called English 101, and the school's required creative thinking class, BRILLIANCE(... as if.)

Any required class has to be lame. The fit-into-the-world classes suck. "Think like me, think like me".....yuck.

I get to play with clay....yea!!!!!

Pottery Rocks!

September 4   8:00-ish pm

LOL...The teacher, Mr. Fine, is going to grade us by the pound.

If we throw 50 pounds of pots we get an "A". He said mistakes are the way we learn. Actually he said, "there is no such thing as mistakes, only learning experiences." "Make lots of pots" is his mantra. Do the work. Feel the clay.

Try new things...new sizes, shapes, widths...keep learning your skills. Your hands remember. Your brain stores info.

I'm using this blog as my self-graded English class. Ms. Keats teaches creative writing and script writing. She wants us to write at least five days per week. Not that grades matter to me, but Mom and Dad will be thrilled I'm making two "A's". Pounds of pots and pounds of words...

My creative thinking teacher, Mr. Bee, is a large man with a huge voice. He teaches the class called "BRILLIANCE," and he really means it. He says I'm smart the way I think, right now, and he isn't trying to change me, only improve my habits.

He has no clue who I am! He's trying to brainwash us. We're the losers at junior college forced to take remedial classes. I don't even know how to spell "remedial," that's how special I am.

He wants us to manage our creativity better so we can make a living as an artist if that's what we want to do. I'm not positive I do, but he wants us to know we can if we're determined to go that route. He's too sure of himself and wrong about me!

Bee said, "If a picture is worth a thousand words, why do we spend so much money educating in words and not in pictures?"

Brilliant....I'm brilliant for the first time, someone says. My teacher said so. Bee teaches animation, so I might not take that class just because he's teaching it. That's really why I'm in school, to be an animator. Life isn't fair. I'm so-o-o not taking Bee for animation next semester. He's supposed to be a great artist, but I can't stand him.

I'll tell my Dad that he's Goth and a lesbian, which should give me an out.

"If a picture is worth a thousand words, why do we spend so much money educating in words and not in pictures?"

My Friend Ginger

September 6   7:08 pm

I ate lunch with Ginger from high school today at the student lounge. She's a few years older, punk with mucho ink and nine visible piercings, which will be a hoot if I want to get Mom amped up. Ginger's rock band has a gig this weekend. I'm going to hear her sing. She's my parents' worst nightmare.J

Ms. Keats says to make your words draw pictures. What is she talking about?

Yes, I still live with Mom and Dad. Lame, but better than homeless or some farmhouse commune. I work part time at Banana Republic. As a freelance artist, really, how can I make a living? That's all my Dad talks about...how're you going to survive as an artist? We fight some, but mostly don't talk. It's easier that way. Mom worries about me in silence.

Inner Male

September 8   2:25 pm

At lunch today, Gingo (that's her stage name) totally hit on this dude at the table next to us. He's gotta be at least 26, buff, and chill. He pounds his laptop every day in the lounge. Someone said he's a writer.

She went right up to his table, sat down and leaned in and said something I couldn't hear. He eyed her up and down then simply said, "Too dark."

I wish I'd recorded it, but the dialogue went something like:

Gingo, "So you like blondes?"

Hottie Guy laughed, then said, "No, your animus is too dark for me."

Gingo said, "What anime? I don't draw Japanese cartoons."

Hottie guy smiled at her and said, "Animus. Animus. Your inner male is dark. Google it."

Gingo got mad at his cryptic dis. Gingo countered with, "Well, your Google is too dark for me."

He laughed. She got up and came back to our table. He went back to his lap-top.

I have no idea what he was talking about, but loved the cool way he said it. I gotta know this guy. He's intense in a way that makes me feel confused and attracted at the same time. Maybe it's just his dark, mysterious eyes that laugh without smiling. What am I saying?

To Think or not to Think

September 11 5:00 pm

Gingo's so hung over I ate lunch by myself today. Last night, I dreamt about Dark eyes from the lounge.   Gingo's coming to school less and less, partying more and more. She says the drugs help her creativity. Maybe they do, but they also help her sleep late and miss more classes.

In BRILLIANCE class, Bee introduced the concepts of "fixed" thinking and "growth" thinking.

Creative minds utilize the growth thinking, non-competitive mindset.

Fixed thinkers categorize, label and try to fit everything in little boxes, and keep them there.

Fixed-sters need to win at everything. They measure themselves constantly in comparison with others.

Mr. Bee reminded us to have balanced lives. Many competitive artists like dancers and actors have limited options for earning money, and they have no life but their art. They often are brilliant, but at a very high price.

Competition isn't bad, but can be a trap. Competition with yourself, the artist you were yesterday, is a healthier head than going against others who you have no control over.

What we think about a thing determines its meaning.

MINDSETS

FACED WITH	FIXED	vs	GROWTH
CHALLENGE	FEAR		EXCITEMENT OPPORTUNITY TO LEARN
NEW SITUATION	THREAT ASSESSMENT		NEW IDEAS & PERSPECTIVES
SCHOOL	PROVE MYSELF		WHERE PROFESSIONALS TEACH ME
OTHER PEOPLE	MEASURING STICKS		PLAYMATES & FRESH PERSPECTIVES
OTHER ARTISTS	COMPETITION		PEER SHARING

There is no intrinsic meaning of things.

We decide meaning for us, not someone else.

That resonates with me.

In fixed thinking, people labeled "smart" always try to prove and re-prove they're smart. Mistakes aren't tolerated by "smart" people.

Learners, creative thinkers, don't have to prove they're smart every step of the way, they just want to learn.

Creatives tolerate mistakes and often are encouraged when they fail to achieve great results when learning happens.

So why's Bee so down on fixed thinking? What's wrong with fixed thinking? I know I'm a "loser". With my grades from "D" to "A", and I don't dress like a Barbie doll, no wonder the mean kids call me "loser". I call them "Mean kids," because they are. Can't Mr. Bee see that I'm dumb? Bee calls me "a learner," not a loser, because I dare to make mistakes. He's more of a loser than I am if he's so blind.

If I label Mr. Dark Eyes "a hottie," isn't that fixed thinking? Tomorrow I'll sit with him and see what kind of growth thinking we can generate. I already labeled him Mr. Dark Eyes. I'm just learning this fixed and growth stuff, give me a break.

On Ellen Degeneres today, Lady Gaga was her guest. Lady Gaga said, "I never felt like I fit in at school. I wasn't a jock, I wasn't an intellectual. There was never a group I felt like I fit in with. I was a weirdo."

She so could have sat with me at lunch.   There were plenty of empty chairs around my Bettie Boop lunch box and me.

Ms. Keats emailed me last night after she read my blog. She wrote what is supposed to be encouragement, "The poem is always perfect when we first think of it. Then converting it to language is the tough part. Practicing on the page is the only way to come close to your initial inspiration."

I think she's saying I'm a bad writer.

Dark Eyes

September 12   1:45 pm

I asked one of the lunch ladies about Mr. Intriguing, but I chickened out of the bold self-intro. Dark Eyes's name is Steven. He likes pizza, chocolate milk, mangos, and drinks tons of water. He's in the film school, taking screenwriting classes and psychology right now. Steven took BRILLIANCE last year. Yes, my opening to his heart, or at least a seat across from him at lunch. We can talk about how doofy the class is.

He looked at me and smiled.   What was that? Maybe he smiled at the girl behind me or had an inspiration for a short story inspired by junior college tater tots that tickled him. I like his smile, and any reason for it is just fine with me.

Process

September 13   12:33 pm

I'm covered in clay dust and schmutz from pottery. No way I'm risking a first impression of poor hygiene and bad hair with Steven. No excuses, I'll meet Steven tomorrow. Pottery class feels right. I lose my sense of time when we're spinning the wheel and I feel the clay in my fingers. All my pots suck, but it's really fun. I'm learning to feel the process of the clay and how to work it, how much water, size of clay ball, wheel speed, finger pressure...

My pots are definitely sucking less, so a creative mindset would say, "way to risk it, to go for it."   Our pottery teacher, Mr. Fine says,

"Don't be attached to results. Learn the process."

Mr. Fine has a creative mindset. He sounds like Mr. Bee with less attitude and volume. Fine even said something about growth thinking.

"Don't be attached to results. Learn the process."

J's Lecture No.1

Thoughts = Behaviors = Results

When people spend lots of money to attend a seminar, they're looking for information to help them get a better understanding or results in some area of study. Pulling from my formal education in Advertising and Psychology and studies on human behavior, I have found that there is a global understanding that people who want to improve their results have to understand:

Thoughts = Behaviors = Results!!!

This idea seems like a very common-sense concept. How people think about things determines their behaviors surrounding the idea or activity and affects the results they get.

How people think and learn about things is related to their attitude or mindset about a subject. If someone has a fixed mindset, or a more inflexible way of thinking about things, they are less likely to accept alternative thoughts, ideas and solutions. These folks often think they know what they need to know about a subject and resist information that conflicts with their own interpretation or experience.

Folks with a growth mindset tend to be open to new perspectives and ideas. Even if they don't necessarily agree with what is being presented, they feel they are richer having heard alternative points of view. Whichever mindset people have, it affects behaviors and thus results.

Changing behaviors is difficult. There is a strong underlying reason why you have adopted the behavior in the first place. Most people are aware that in order to lose weight and stay fit, you need to exercise and watch what and how much you eat. So having the information, alone, isn't really enough. Some people will try to tackle the behavior head on, join a gym and/or follow the latest diet. Many people who don't get the results they want actually did change their behaviors, but their thoughts underlying their behaviors didn't change, so they wound up falling into their old routine and habits.

While I think most people like to say they want things to change in their lives, often their behaviors don't support what they are saying. I tell my students, "If you want to change the way things are, you have to change." I then tell them, "If you want to get the same results as most people, you only have to do what most people do." Unfortunately, most people aren't doing their dream job or achieving the goals and success they want in life. If you want to achieve the same results as successful people, you have to think and act like a successful person.

So what are you waiting for? Seek out some successful people who are doing what you want to do. Read biographies on the lives of successful people to find out how they think and how they handled difficulties. Find out what behaviors they adopted and stuck to in order to achieve the results they ultimately achieved. Without fail you will probably discover the road to success was difficult and involved a great deal of work and perseverance. Shake off that fear and seek out a role model or mentor today!!!

MINDSET Exercise

List three areas where you have a growth mindset.

1. _______________________________________

2. _______________________________________

3. _______________________________________

List three areas where you have a fixed mindset.

1. _______________________________________

2. _______________________________________

3. _______________________________________

OMG

September 14 7:48 pm

OMG (Oh My God) Ms. Keats wants me to spell out the text lingo.

Steven is the coolest person I've ever met. I love how he thinks. It's all about the life quest with him. His life is a journey with fellow travelers he meets teaching him lessons along the way. He thinks I'm a fellow traveler and we have things to teach each other. What can he possibly find interesting about me? I draw, paint, and live with my parents. I better start taking my journey a little more seriously if I'm to be a worthy fellow traveler.

An artist is on a journey of self-discovery. Why did I get sweaty around him? A good place to start is discovering why I get sweaty palms and pits around Steven.

Emoticons are symbols that show feelings. For the non-tweeters and those over 30, here is a key. Wikipedia says, "Western style is written most often from left to right. Thus, most commonly, one will see the eyes on the left, followed by nose and mouth."

Tilt your head to the left, it'll show you a face.

:-)   Smiling

: - D   Laughing

; -)   Wink

: - O   Surprise, shock

( )   Hug, or Cyberhug

> : (Angry, mad

Seeded Thoughts

September 15 8:55 pm

Steven can't be the reason I'm doing anything. I'll have my journey with or without him. Oh, please God, let it be with him for at least a semester or until I see him with his shirt off. My legs are shaking. What's the matter with me?

In BRILLIANCE today, we studied a chapter from the book, <u>VIRUS OF THE MIND</u> by Richard Brodie. Mr. Bee's thrust for the day was that "all thoughts are generated by brains", therefore:

No thoughts are true with a capital "T".

We learned about our thoughts and where they come from. There is "thought science." It's called Memetics.

Thoughts have seeds called memes, just like our bodies have seeds called genes.

The study of memes is memetics, the science of thought replication.

MEMES

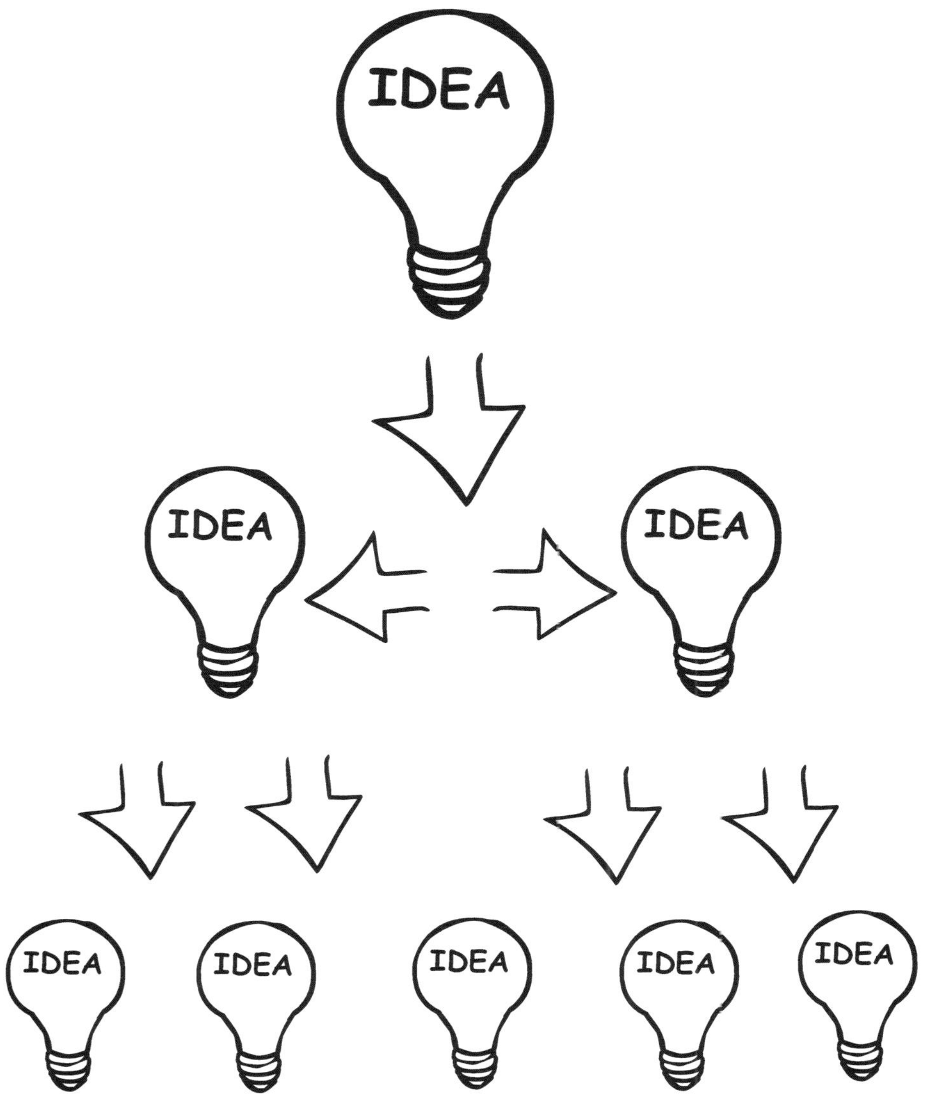

No thoughts are true with a capital "T".

The study of genes is genetics, the science of cell replication.

The main goal of a gene and a meme is survival at any cost. Truth is irrelevant.

A good meme or gene is one that survives. It has nothing to do with morality. "Good" means survivability.

All thoughts are generated by brains. No thought is true to the exclusion of other thoughts.

At lunch, I started complaining about BRILLIANCE. Steven jumped right in and enthusiastically asked what we were learning. Class was interesting today and thank God I listened. Steven loved that I knew about memes. He loved BRILLIANCE last year when he took it. Am I too harsh on Mr. Bee?

Advertisers, religions, governments, and parents all try to pass their (memes) thoughts into other people for sales, loyalty, or so we'll behave during and after school.

This thought science really makes sense to me. The material is relevant. Maybe I'm labeling Mr. Bee too quickly and being all fixed thinking about him?

GENES

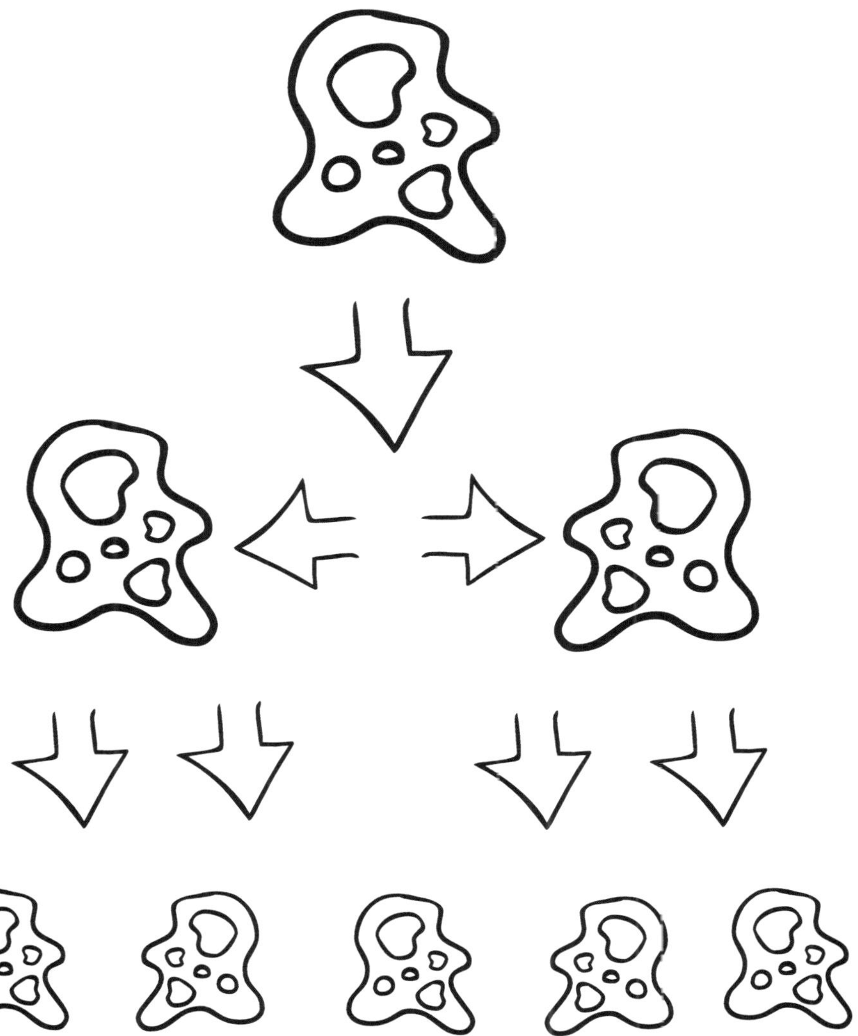

If I adopt the memes of others, I'm in their group. If I don't adopt
their memes, that makes me either their enemy or a potential convert,
someone to be destroyed, or subjugated.

Within memes, part of their message is that other thoughts are bad or
wrong or not as good, thus self-perpetuating themselves as superior
thoughts, superior memes.

All thoughts are self-sustaining propaganda.

Examples:

Religions that preach they're the only true path to eternal bliss.

"Blondes have more fun". (Be blonde, be happier)

Steven added, "Memes are neither good nor bad morally. Thoughts are
not good or bad. Memes are just memes, as viruses or sharks are not
evil, simply genetically designed to do what they do.

Survival is everything, even though their survival might result in the
death of a host body (virus) or Pacific coast surfer (shark)...not from
malice, but from natural self-survival of that genetic imperative."
Memes survive by:

Propagation

Regeneration and

Mutation

All memes and genes strive for long lasting life – their prime directive.
When conscious, we get to choose which memes we plug into our
consciousness.

The key is being conscious of which memes we adopt. We have choice
of our thoughts.

"Recognizing that there is a battle for our minds precedes our ability to choose."

~ Richard Brodie

Meme Exercise I

List five memes (true or false, doesn't matter.)

1. _______________________________________

2. _______________________________________

3. _______________________________________

4. _______________________________________

5. _______________________________________

Alec

September 14 9:14 pm

I'd seen him sit with Steven before, so it came as no surprise that Alec
joined us for lunch today. As quiet and reflective as Steven is, that's how
extraverted Alec is. He may be the funniest person I've ever met. OMG...I
spit soda at least twice today when he went on and on about wardrobe
choices in the room. If possible, Alec is slightly gayer than Curt on
Glee, and has a comic mania of Dane Cook. Choreographer Adam
Shankman is his idol. Alec's a triple threat. Dancer-singer-actor. : - D

I cannot wait to see him in a show. I never cared for catty before,
but this little queen made me appreciate fashion and meanness like
never before. He called me Lisa Marie meets Salvation Army, which is
exactly what I've been going for. Oh, to be seen as I see myself!

Alec is my new best girlfriend. Gingo is M.I.A., (missing in action).

<u>J's Lecture No.2</u>

How to get good at anything?

I go to comic book conventions and sit with friends in their booths. We listen to people wanting to get into the industry who stop by, show their portfolio and ask questions. One out of three folks will inevitably say something like, "Wow, you are so good! How did you learn how to draw so well?" My friends will almost always reply, "I draw all the time." Many look disappointed and respond almost as if they have been brushed off, "No, I mean… what's your secret? How did you get so good? My friends say, "I draw 8 to 10 hours a day. That's how I got good."

Over the years I have come up with a three step formula that I think is easy to remember that I share with my students on how to get good at anything. I even make my students repeat the steps out loud in class:

PRACTICE, PRACTICE, PRACTICE…

RESEARCH, RESEARCH, RESEARCH…

NETWORK, NETWORK, NETWORK.

Meaty Thoughts

Ms. Keats likes my blog, yet wants it less social and with more "meat" as she calls it. Asking a vegetarian for more meat, now that's funny. My meme of how to eat healthy and responsibly is meat-averse, but I get her drift. My friends have meaty thoughts too, so I'm including some of them.

Ms. Keats wrote me back saying, "Art is like beginning a joke before you know the punch line."

She thinks of writing as art, her art. I never really looked at it that way. Drawing is art. Music is art. Acting is too. She actually writes screenplays on her own. Steven is in her script writing class and loves her.

At lunch today, I asked Steven why so many guys are into video games.

Fantasy can be healthy according to Steven. Video games can be healthy, even the violent ones. Jung wrote about archetypes, the universal symbols that every culture seems to conjure up in some way. Father, warrior, mother, clown, banker...the whole deck of tarot cards really. Everyone can supposedly tap into archetypes in our dreams and in our outer worlds. His film class studied STAR WARS as a great example of tapping into universal themes and developing characters.

The shy kid who plays Warrior Kong and learns that he can defeat monsters engages his inner warrior. Then in his outer world he begins to develop his real assertiveness, beyond the fantasy where he exercised that part of himself. He practiced in a safe environment, then brought it to the world. Do archetypes really exist? Cultures around the world come up with archetypes separately. Are some thoughts universal, or at least human constructs of universality? I have no idea. Some memes say yes.

All thoughts are generated by brains, so none can be "THE TRUTH".

Meme Exercise II

List five memes that guide your life

1. _______________________________________

2. _______________________________________

3. _______________________________________

4. _______________________________________

5. _______________________________________

Ms. Payne

Alec is in a stage play. He's the second lead, playing the best friend.
The director loves him and only occasionally has to ask him to tone it
down. Easier to tone down than bring up expressiveness. Alec also
butched-it-up from what he tells us. I'll believe that when I see it. ; -)

Steven says we all are in our own constructs of a life that plays out like
our own movie. Shakespeare said, "The world is a stage." Alec's in my
personal show playing my new best friend.

Brain biology we're getting in BRILLIANCE follows the memes info
naturally. Bee makes sense even though he's too loud and cocky. I do
agree with his statement:

As an artist, I need to know how my mind works.

I cared nothing for science until Ms. Payne's biology class in junior
high. She loved her subject so much it was infectious. Plus, she let me
draw the cells, the organs, and animals for extra credit.

I learned a ton from drawing body parts. I saw inside myself, my body
and how it works as if for the first time. Visually, I got it. I haven't
cared much for science since. Now, I like it again.

I connected with Ms. Payne and I cared what she thought about me
and my work. I wanted to please her. Why is that? I learned because I
had fun and I loved her. How? Why? Science is science, but it was fun
that year. Who am I?

Mr. Bee is so arrogant. He's too sure of himself and that annoys me.
The information about my mind, he's so wrong. He doesn't know me.
He did give me an assignment to draw the brain, which is fun. Not
everyone, just me. Why did he pick on me?

"Evolution" is a meme, not the truth. We'll explore evolution anyway.

Humans dwell at the top of the thought chain because of our brain
development.

3 BRAIN THEORY

HUMAN

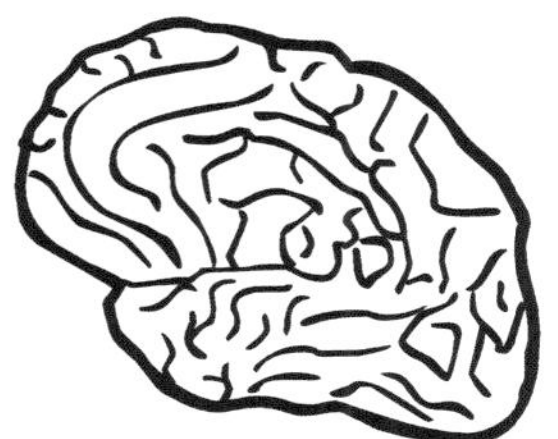

MAMMAL

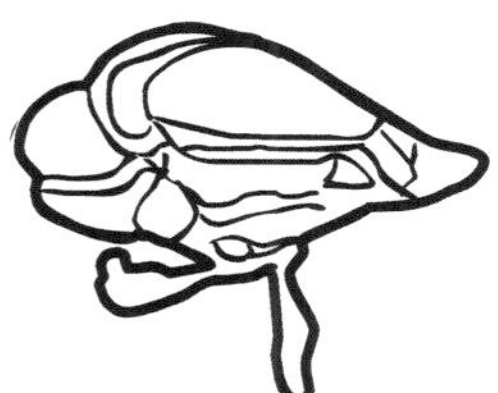

LIZARD

All brains, human and animal, have basic parts to handle breathing, hormone secreting, and other unconscious functions. Imagine if we had to think every time we breathed. Even the dumbest creatures have brains.

The most basic brain part, the brain stem, is nearly the same in lizards as it is in humans.

This reptile part handles automatic actions such as breathing, heart rate, sleeping, and waking up. This part functions all the time, unconsciously, even when we sleep, or we'd just die.

Sitting on top of our reptilian brain is what we share with mammals. This mammalian brain handles the four "f's" – fight, flight, feeding, and ....finding a mate. These functions are handled in this reactive brain part and are referred to as instinctual behaviors.

We could call fraternities the Four F club, beer not required. Beer just makes sure these guys have no higher thoughts.   God, I sound judgmental. Enough for tonight.

Brainiac

September 22 9:46 pm

Mr. Fine was funny today, but right on. He said, "Most artists dream of having made great work, not the process of making the great work. The amount of time it takes to actually make the art would be way too long for a daydream."

Okay then, females have the same brains as men, so we have the four f's, too. "Judging" is from a fixed mindset about good and bad, smart and dumb and putting things in a rigid box. Learning is best done from a growth mindset. I got all fixy-brained about boys and men. It's even fixed thinking for me to think I'm dumb or a loser. In growth thinking, I'm not dumb or a loser, or smart, or a winner.   I'm Mary and I like to learn. I make mistakes while learning, but so what, that's how I learn.

Oh, no! Bee is getting inside my head with help from Fine.

The mammal brain has a part called the amygdala that emotions come from. Rage, fear, pleasure and memories of these feelings are triggered in the amygdala. (See my drawing)

The hippocampus converts short term memories to long-term ones. Some people are better than others based on the size of this part. (See my brain drawing)

The thalamus connects to all of our senses and sits right in the middle of this second brain. We'd be a block of wood without these mammal parts. Well, maybe just a lizard with no emotions, feelings or higher thoughts.

Higher thoughts come from our human brain. This third part is a very thin layer of tissue that sits on top of our reptile and mammal brains. I saw my sister's sonograms before she had Emily. Emily looked like a lizard, then a mammal, and now a human.

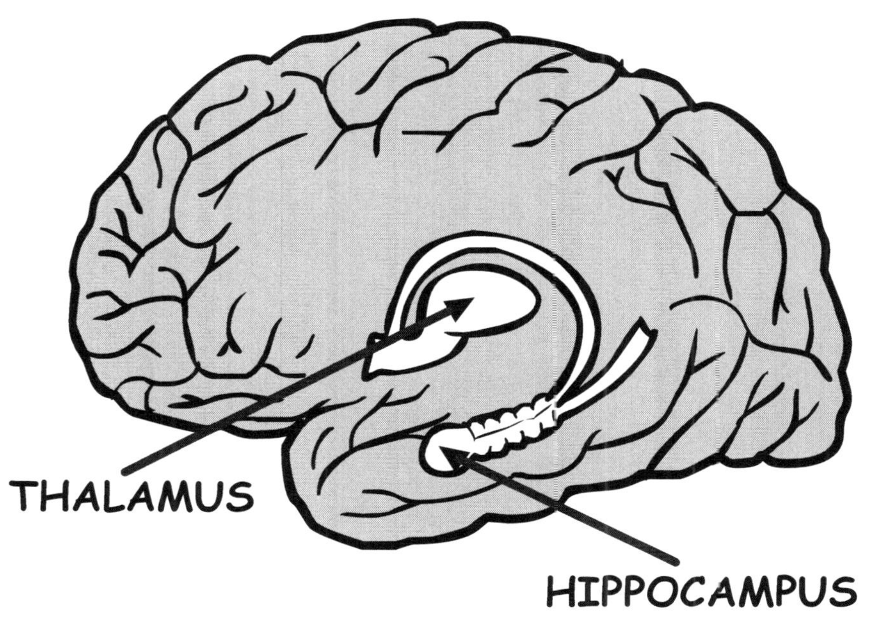

Automatic actions – Unconscious

Reactive actions – Instinctive

Human actions – Conscious choice

Brain development continues after birth well into our late 20's...
and why Gingo is such a dumb-ass for doing drugs. Our brain's
development is altered by chemicals we generate hormonally, and from
the outside, pharmaceutically.

Neural pathways develop throughout our entire lives if we have a
growth mindset and are trying new things and failing and learning and
not calling yourself a loser when you fail.

I got Judgey again, sorry,...fixed thinking about Gingo. I'll stop writing
until I can behave better. : - (

Exercise – Brain Questions

Do you have to think to breathe? _______

Do you have to think to feel? _______

Do you have to think to create? _______

What is the priority of your body – breathing,
feeling, or creating? _______

Who needs condiments?

Steven asked me out on a date, well, at least for a sandwich off campus.
A sandwich date!!! Be cool. Don't scare him. Don't scare myself.
What'll I wear? It's just a sandwich. What if I get mayo, or worse,
mustard on my blouse? No condiments.   I'll have a dry sandwich.
Alec performs next weekend and Steven and I will certainly go
together.

I made my first good pot today. I don't suck. I do have 25 pounds of
pots that do suck. I am not my pots. I have one good pot. I now know
how to make good pots. It wasn't luck. I learned how and I can repeat
that good behavior. That's what Mr. Fine says anyway:

"Growth thinking embraces the process."

Fixed thinking cares only for the results.

Growth thinking is more joyful and gets better results in the long run
anyway.   : -)

I swear Bee and Fine must be friends, or there is an artistic way of
living that BRILLIANCE has figured out how to teach?

Gingo looked terrible today. She thinks Alec is "too queer to be near".
I like Alec better than her, and he doesn't smell like cigarettes and beer.
When I told her that, she got mad at me. I laughed at myself when I
told her that "her process" bothers me. She had no idea what I meant.

"Growth thinking embraces the process."

No straight lines!

The human part of our brain, the "cortex," develops only after the reptile and mammal parts develop to support the cortex. The thin layered cortex is creviced and folded, divided into in two halves.

Our cortex is a meandering, winding landscape of valleys and ridges and crevices of tissue.   Nothing is straight-lined on the cortex.   Why then does school use straight rows of text and numbers when our physical brain has no straight lines for storage?

Our cortex has no straight rows, so there must be a better way to teach and store info than rows and straight lines.

Mind mapping is a way to order information more closely to the way we actually store it, in little packets strewn about the irregular landscape of the cortex.

<u>The Mind Mapping Book</u> by brothers Tony and Barry Buzan is required reading for BRILLIANCE, and surprisingly emotional for me. I cried when I saw how they do mind maps. It's what I've been doing for years and getting punished for it.

Creative IQ can now be measured in large part due to the work of these mind-mapping pioneers, my newest heroes. They're measured creative geniuses and have taught mind mapping at English schools, major corporations, and international think tanks for decades.

Why didn't I know about mind mapping until now? Maybe my own belittled inventions are more brilliant than the fixed, straight line thinkers in high school. Mr. Bee gave us some good information. He must not be as bad as I thought. At least he cares about artists and creative thinkers and how we've been misdiagnosed our whole lives.

Fact memorization is one form of intelligence, and it's the easiest to test for. Bee says there are at least six kinds of intelligence, probably more. Creative, physical, emotional, maybe spatial, shapes, orangutans, and rhinos...I forgot the others...and why I test so poorly for memory stuff!!!

Memory regurgitation is just one form of intelligence and why Bee designed BRILLIANCE, to explore other ways of thinking besides what he calls "Academic Bulimia." He designed the course? Hmmm... Maybe I underestimated this man?

We store info in nooks, crannies, and all over the place.

The brain isn't an extremely well ordered file system with neat rows and tiers.

(This is why it's so hard for neuro-scientists to map brains.)

J's Lecture No.3

PRACTICE, PRACTICE, PRACTICE

Success takes discipline and practice. I think a lot of people don't want to hear that it takes a lot of work and time to get results. In Malcolm Gladwell's book, Outliers, he suggests from his study of successful people that it takes about 10,000 hours to master a skill. The master animator, Chuck Jones, said his teacher in art school told him, "We all have at least 100,000 bad drawings inside of us. The sooner we get them out and onto paper, the sooner we'll get to the good ones buried deep within."

Habits are developed from the activities we do most often. It has been said that when legendary basketball player, Larry Bird, was asked to shoot a commercial where he missed the basket from the free throw line, it took him a number of tries just to miss the basket. So, if you want to get good at something, the first step is to PRACTICE, PRACTICE, PRACTICE.

Information storage varies from person to person, from brain to brain.

Linear thinking - finding the best sequences.

Radiant thinking - finding the most connections.

Bee opened to the chapter on Mind Mapping. Mind mapping explores connections of thoughts in what is called radiant thinking.

Radiant thinking shows connections of our thoughts.

Bee put together a mind map for his course, BRILLIANCE.

MIND MAPPING

Mind Maps explore connections

MIND MAPS USE RADIANT PROCESS

In evolutionary terms, we're infants, still evolving physically and in our processes.

The brain's natural architecture today processes by:

> Receiving
>
> Holding
>
> Outputting
>
> Analyzing
>
> Controlling

Radiant Thinking – connecting

Use a mind map for taking notes radiantly.

FOR MIND MAPPING:

KEY WORDS – make them Bigger

Standout Colors – Brighter

Efficiency – Important

STIMULATE THE BRAIN

In a Mind Map, have a Central Image

Mind Map Exercise:

Draw a Mind Map of your own Happiness
(ME in the center)

We all learn and retain differently.

Reminder: Uniqueness of individuals, unique associations and applications of words and thoughts. Your mind map is designed for you, by you, not right or wrong.

85 to 98% of people recall a picture...why it's smart to use pictures in mind map notes and thoughts.

In a Mind Map, have a Central Image

Images are universal, words are not.

Pictures are better absorbed and retained than words.

Damaging Myths about pictures:

1.   Images and colors are primitive, childish, immature and irrelevant

2.   The power to create and reproduce images is a god given talent of a tiny minority.

Brilliance Truth is:
Everyone can draw and improve visual presentations with practice.

Images are universal, words are not.

Pictures are better absorbed and retained than words.

J's Lecture No.4

RESEARCH, RESEARCH, RESEARCH

When I assign projects in my classes I tell my students the first thing they need to do before they start a project is do the research. I can always tell when my students haven't done their research on a project. Normally, there is something about the project that just doesn't ring true.

Almost all of the great painters in history have used references and found inspiration in each other's work. Writers are taught to write about what they know. Animators are told to observe real life or videos to see how people, animals and objects move.

One day, years ago, I was hanging out with my good friend Dan Kuenster, an ex-Disney animator who went on to direct a number of films at Don Bluth Studios and later won an Emmy for storyboarding on an independent project he did. Dan is one of the most talented and fastest artists I know.

As I was sitting in a room with him, he was asked by another person to draw something. The first thing he did was jump on the Internet and look up pictures of the object for reference. I knew Dan could have come up with something out of his head – I've seen boxes filled with thousands of drawings he has done – but he didn't do that. He wanted to do his homework first by doing the necessary research. It was that day that I decided; if it was good enough for Dan, it was good enough for me. I have learned in the years since that the best creatives always do their research.

For mind mapping:

Use a central image instead of a central word

Advantages of Mind mapping for note taking:

1. Saves time - relevant words only
2. Review quicker
3. Key words
4. Concentration on real issues
5. Style more remember-able
6. Clearer associations
7. Stimulated brain remembers and associates
8. New thoughts stimulated
9. Keeps you alert and receptive

Radiant Thinking

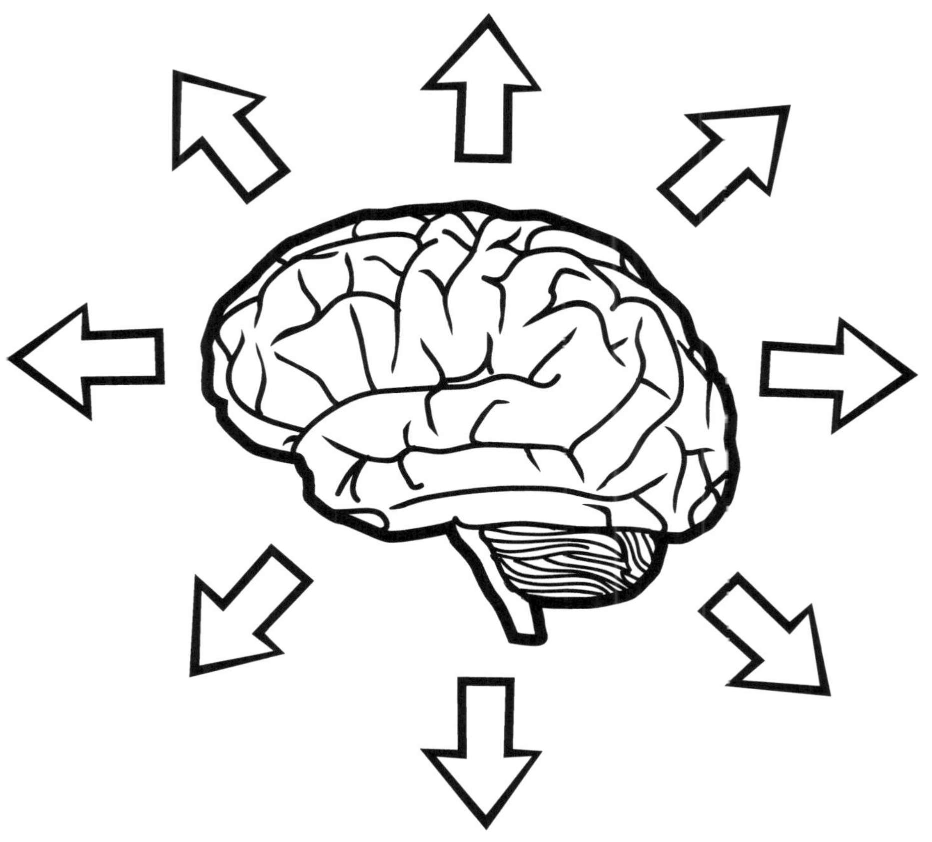

Language is a narrow form of expression.

Freedom is not chaos

1. Law of Technique in mind mapping
        Use emphasis
        Use association
        Clarity
        Personal style

2. Law of Lay-out in mind mapping
        Hierarchy
        Numerical order

A central image focuses the eye and the brain

Other Tools for Mind Mapping:

Freedom is not chaos.

Use kinesthetic, other senses, physical sensations, movement, images

BIG
    Medium
        Small
            Tiny

1. Print (not cursive)

2. Spacing

3. Codes-symbols

4. One word per line

5. Connect lines to other lines

Thicker lines more meaningful

Central lines

Create Boundaries

Chunking – we generally store no more than 7 bits of info, so minimize.

Horizontal page better for drawing

Brains enjoy and prefer

1) order

2) numbers

3) hierarchy

4) chronology

5) order of importance.

Develop your own personal style

Practice Mind Mapping

The birth of BRILLIANCE in a mind map:

Create a Central Image and label it.

Define important subjects supporting and explaining the central image. For Brilliance:

Biology of the brain.

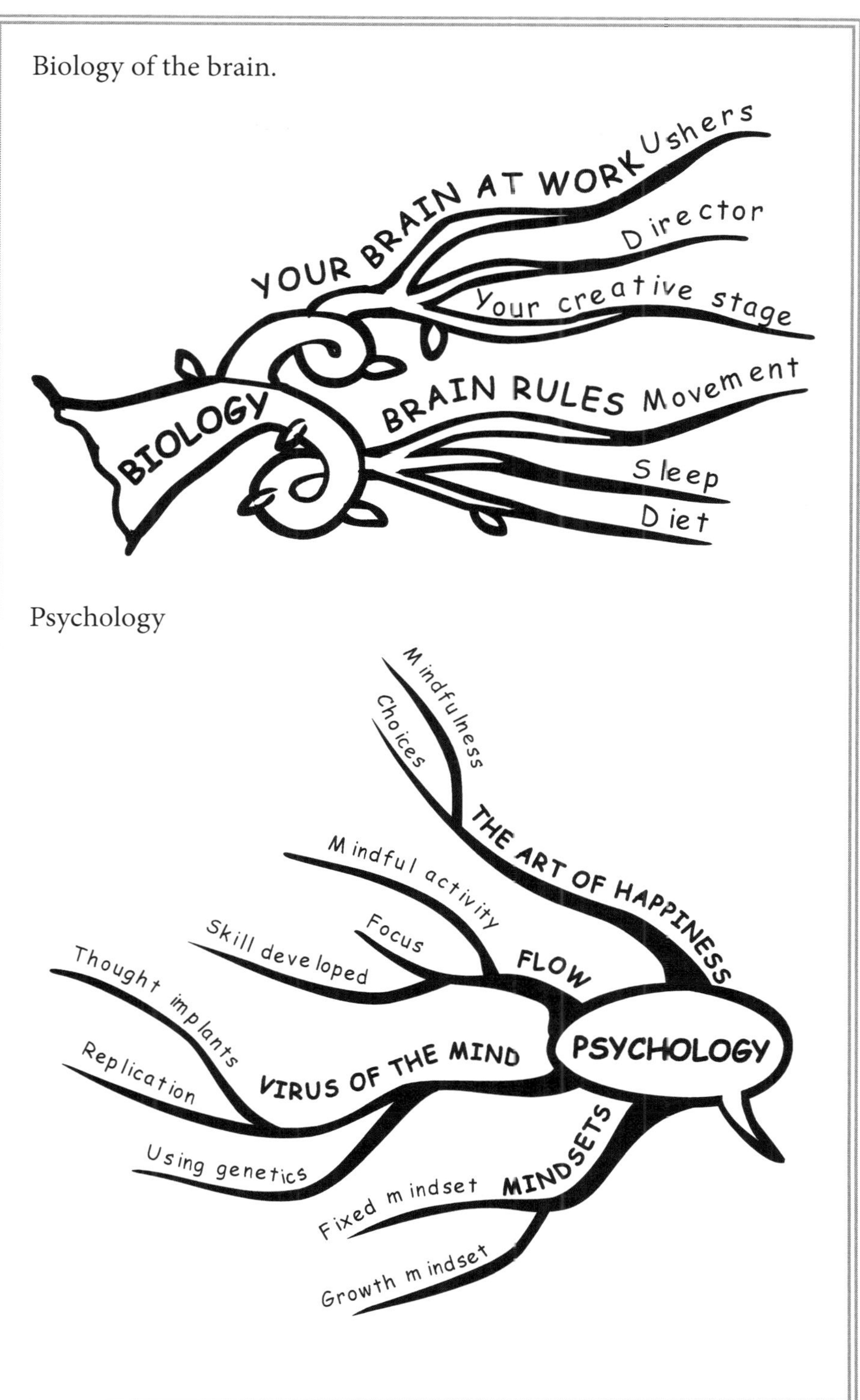

Psychology

Thinking Styles

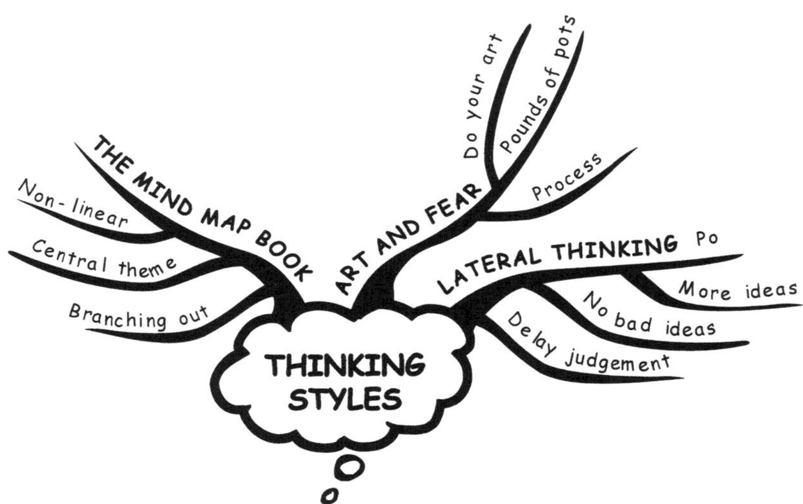

Our mind map of the book BRILLIANCE, UNDERSTANDING
THE CREATIVE MIND.

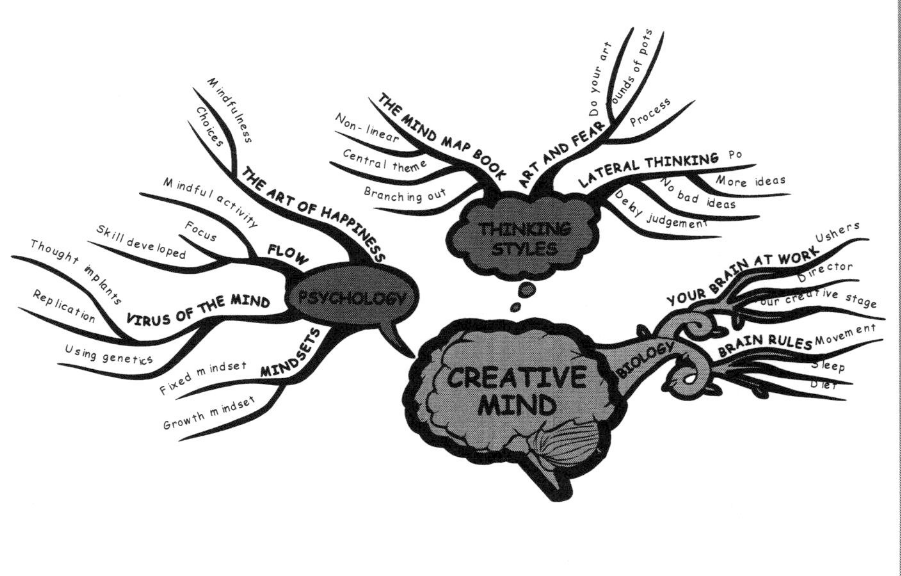

Mind Map Exercise:

List five areas where mind maps can be useful.

1. _______________________________________

2. _______________________________________

3. _______________________________________

4. _______________________________________

5. _______________________________________

Wordsmith

Oddly, Ms. Keats rather enjoyed all the picture talk even though her artistry is as a "wordsmith" as she calls herself. Visual arts don't compete, but actually enhance her work. She writes me little streamlined notes that are artistic in their directness. Today's note:

"People who need certainty in their lives are less likely to do art that is risky. Uncertainty is a constant companion for an artist, and your ability to handle uncertainty is a large part in deciding your success."

I get sidetracked easily by drawing and other fun things. We store short term and long term memories, facts, and emotions in the folds and recesses of our brains.

No two brains are exactly alike and that's why two people often experience the same event with different emotions and memories.

Our base of thoughts exerts influence with what we do with the new information.

How we treat new information depends on what's already in our brains and memories.

Relational – how does this new thought relate to what I feel is true?

Associative – what do we associate with the new info?

I put Steven's intense brown eyes in a different category than say Alec would, well, maybe that's a bad example...let's just say we all prioritize info individually.

The sandwich date was fun and exhausting. Steven is minoring in psychology. He went on about the anima, animus, the shadow, and self. Then, from a gaming class he took, we talked about Star Wars, archetypes, and how our inner effects our outer. Video games rely on these forces for their characters and missions.

The "anima" is the inner female in males. How men act towards

How we
treat new
information
depends on
what's already
in our brains
and memories.

women in the outer world shows their inner female...awe, fear, revulsion, tenderness, jealousy...all female qualities in differing amounts and intensity, all challenges for men to resolve by dealing with their inner and outer females. Huge for building characters in his scripts!!!

Women and men have anima and animus, or female and male complexes, inside their psyches. Wow, it was intense. The inner male, "the animus," rhymes with penis, that's what he saw in Ginger that turned him off. She was too angry in her inner male side to embrace the tender male that he was.

Her inner male was a mismatch for his outer male.

He saw that right away by her presentation, outfits, brashness, yet without judgment, it seemed. He's so awesome. Her male inner parts were too rough for him.

Anima rhymes with vagina, the inner female.

Animus rhymes with penis, the inner male.

He talked about sex a lot without talking about sex. I was overwhelmed with listening, thinking, sweating, and over-chewing my dry sandwich. I had three lemonades just to finish lunch. I so wanted mayo or dressing on that dry cucumber, avocado desert pita. My salivary glands are sore from making extra saliva. I may have avoided wetness on my sandwich, but not on my sweaty training bra. I still wear a tween bra and I'm twenty-one. Why do I care about sex? Why do men love big breasts? He bought me and my small breasts a sandwich. It must be love.

Talking with Steven about sex...OMG (oh My God), and we have inner sex parts, too!! Does my inner male match his outer?

Our "shadow" is that part of ourselves that we're unaware of. Our anima and animus that live in the shadows control our behavior unconsciously.

Consciousness, awareness is a big deal. Our unconscious stays active
and controls behavior without our knowing. Our actual lives reflect
both our conscious and unconscious choices. That's the best way to see
how conscious we are, by what's in our lives. As they say, the proof is in
the pudding. How does it taste?

The shadow, what we don't know about ourselves is really powerful,
especially when we sabotage our relationships, our careers, or even
say stupid things or get depressed and don't know why. No mayo or
dressing... I was pretty conscious at lunch of how messy I can be when
I'm nervous. This BRILLIANCE class might be rubbing off on me. The
condiments did not rub off on my blouse. Enough about me!

Steven says his journey for inner wisdom shows up in his outer life. He
can tell what's going inside by looking at the results in his outer world.
His success, his relationships... his journey, his discovery, all reflect the
thoughts onto the outer screen, the movie he's living...It's heavy and
moist being with him. I showered when I got home and took a nap.

Does the order we learn things affect how we react to new input?

Mr. Bee says that most people have more unconscious (subconscious,
same thing) thoughts controlling their behavior than conscious
thoughts. Like an iceberg, more is below the surface of our awareness.

The goal is to become more conscious of why we do what we do so
we can change where we want to...enhance the positives, reduce and
eliminate negativities.

The goal of BRILLIANCE is to create more awareness of what we think
and how we think.

ICEBERG THEORY

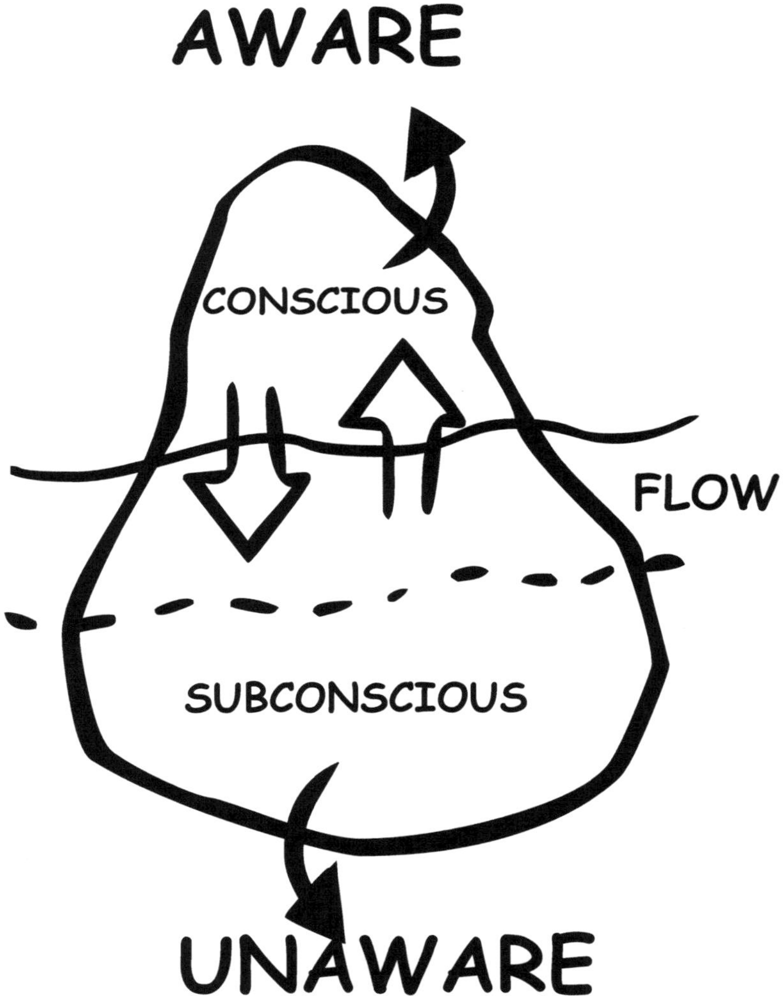

The goal of
BRILLIANCE is
to create more
awareness of
what we think
and how we
think.

<u>J's Lecture No.5</u>

NETWORK, NETWORK, NETWORK

A lot of the creatives I know are cave dwellers. They like to work by themselves in dark corners. If they have to work in an office environment, they un-plug from the world by listening to music or remove themselves from the world around them as much as possible.

I have personally seen examples of amazingly talented creatives who are working various odd jobs because they can't find a job in which someone will pay them for their creative skills. I have seen other less exceptional artists who are constantly in demand and working all the time. Why? Because they know how to network.

I constantly tell my students, "Who you know will get you in the door. What you know will keep you there." People mostly hire people they know and like. That's why most employers will often put referrals at the top of the stack. So how do you get to know people? Get involved.

Five ways to get involved: 1) Take a class, 2) Join a professional organization, 3) Volunteer, 4) Get an Internship, and 5) Find a mentor.

Take a Class – One of the best and easiest ways to get involved and meet people is to take a class in your craft. Often, your local university or community college will offer classes. This is a great way to meet other people interested in what you are interested in. Here, you'll find professors eager to help interested people.

I highly recommend taking a class taught by an adjunct professor. These adjunct professors are often practicing or retired professionals who have years of experience in the field. Sometimes, they are business owners who are also on the lookout for bright and talented students to hire.

Join a professional organization – professional organizations are great places to meet like-minded folks who are typically doing what you want to do. The downside to professional organizations is that many of them require you to be a professional to join. However, if you are a student, they often have student memberships and mentoring programs.

If you join a professional organization, don't just show up to the meetings and sit with the same people every week. Ask to join one of the committees and get involved. The surest way to successfully network is to show people your willingness to help.

What if there are no apt professional organizations in town? Start one. That's what I did. Find other people in town who do what you want to do. Then find a regular place to meet. It could be Denny's or the local church. Pick a goal or something to accomplish and then chart your progress. You will be surprised how quickly word will spread and the two or three people you started off with could turn into 30 or even 300.

Volunteer – If you just don't have the money to take a class, or pay a fee to join a professional organization, then the next step is to find a non-profit community organization that might be in need of your talents. Non-profits are always looking for good volunteers. As people get to know you and you have started to make yourself a valuable and dependable volunteer, the people in charge will inevitably ask you what your goals are and how they might be able to help you. They may introduce you to people they know who also need your talents. If you do get an opportunity that works out, don't just quit the organization. That could come back to haunt you some day. More on that in another lecture.

Get an Internship – If you can get one, an internship is an excellent way to learn valuable on-the-job training. These opportunities are golden and may be difficult to obtain. Often, internships actually cost companies time and money. Many of my students have complained to me that they are just being used for free or cheap labor. Although that may be true, they are not taking into account the lost time and productivity of the company when people are tasked to train, monitor, or even fix the mistakes of an intern.

So how do you get an internship? Normally, yes, you guessed it... you have to either know someone or be really, really, really talented. If you are exceptionally talented companies may give you an opportunity to show them what you can do and see how well you fit into the existing culture.

If you are not exceptionally talented, like in my situation, it can be a matter of timing. Sometimes when companies get into a position where they need extra help, anyone will do. If you do a great job, are dependable, and get along with everyone, they may hire you or refer you to another business that is looking for a new employee.

5) Find a Mentor – Finding a mentor is one of the best career moves you can make. Most great mentors have lots of experience in your desired field. However, regardless of the level of experience, a great mentor will be someone who supports and guides you as you work to achieve your goals and dreams. I, personally, think some of the best mentors give you enough freedom to fall down and fail, but are there to lend a hand and give direction while you are dusting yourself off.

50 cent

For some reason, I got a 50 cent raise at Banana Republic. My Dad is way prouder of my raise from precise jean folding and diligent blouse hanging than my two good pots or learning that I'm brilliant. He just shakes his head that his artist daughter could say those words out loud, "I'm brilliant." Mom made a big deal out of my pots.   One of them is a berry strainer that she used today for her morning blueberries. She's sweet, but I can tell she's worried about me, too.

Steven told me about his big brother, Jeff, who speaks with a horrible stutter. Jeff's a math genius, studying at M.I.T. Although he is able to bring information in easily, he has a brutal time outputting the info through speech. Alec is the exact opposite – able to express any thought or expression easily, but he's dyslexic and slow to learn (input) new info. Steven loved Brilliance because it showed him that individual brains have different strengths and weaknesses.

Mr. Fine laid another Fine-ism on us today:

"Talent is a trap. No one cares about your talent, only the art you produce."

PART II

Piece o' Cake

The icing on the cake of our brain is our cerebral cortex. It's about as thick as icing, and literally sits on top of our mammal brain, the cake. After our lower brains develop (the reptile and mammal parts), then this human top layer forms. This cortex tissue is made up of more complex brain cells and neural networks (our wiring) that make up this top layer. We need the cake to support the icing.

Brain development has a scientific order...first is survival, then emotions develop, and lastly, intellect is formed.

The brain's development fits with Maslow's psychological hierarchy-of-needs pyramid. From his 1943, A Theory of Human Motivation, Abraham Maslow studied the best and brightest, from Einstein to Eleanor Roosevelt. His theories on psychology pre-dated modern brain research and match up perfectly with what brain science has uncovered. Getting your basic needs met is a priority before you can do your best work.

Self-actualization: Morality, creativity, spontaneity, problem solving, lack of prejudice, acceptance happens only when the lower needs are met.

Esteem: Self-esteem, confidence, achievement, respect of others, respect by others.

Love/belonging: Friendship, family, sexual intimacy.

Safety: Security of body, employment, health, property.

Physiological: Breathing, food, water, sex, sleep, excretion.

Maslow's Hierarchy of Needs

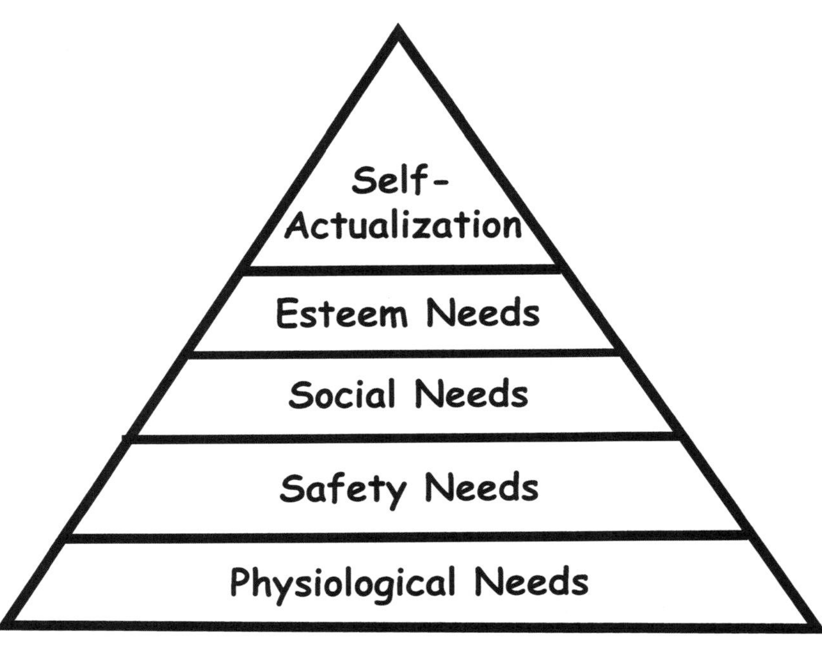

Self-actualization only happens when the lower levels are satisfied. Lower doesn't mean less important.

Priorities:
> First SURVIVAL
> Then EMOTIONS
> Then INTELLECT

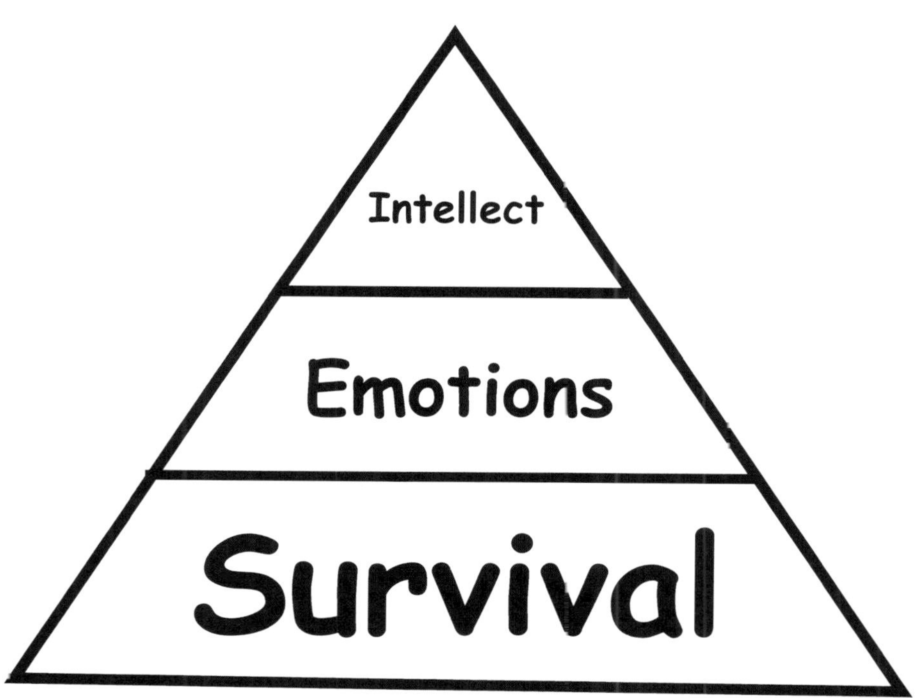

As the last part to develop, the cortex is sustained by the underlying brain. The cortex is not more important for survival, but is more important for higher functioning, learning, and being an active processor of new information.

The cortex buzzes with electric pulses and waves of activity. Depending on what we're learning, storing or retrieving from our files, different parts are more engaged than others. The area located behind the forehead is where we combine information in different ways.
This idea-combining area is called the "Pre-Frontal Cortex" or PFC.

Artists, the pre-frontal cortex is where the action happens, the "pfc" is where we create.

Everything we're learning in Brilliance is to better understand and engage with this creative, temperamental, and huge energy-consuming part of the brain – the PFC.

Mr. Bee calls the PFC our performance stage. It's where we bring in thoughts (actors), and see how they work with other thoughts (actors). Whatever your art, when you create something new and different, conception happens in your PFC.

Thoughts impregnate, mutate, meld, morph, and change each other in this area of the brain called the PFC.

On our stage, we bring in new and old info and combine them in new ways, holding several thoughts in the PFC at once for their chemistry to reveal itself, or not. This area must be a safe place for the sensitive actors who're shy, vulnerable, and fleeting, like actors auditioning for roles. Uncertain what the director wants of them, they show up and stay only so long as they're valued. Often, even the director doesn't know until he's seen interactions of multiple actors together what the new play, song, or drawing will look like.

Overall brain function greatly affects how well the director can do his job, and why we're paying attention to the whole brain in Brilliance, not just the PFC.

We're only able to send energy to this creative area, when survival and emotional areas aren't clamoring for attention.

All this icing talk, I'll be right back after a Hostess cupcake fix.

Yummmmmmmy!! Much better.

Our brain requires lots of energy. That's why we get hungry for quick sugar fixes when we're working at thinking... (you like how I made my sugar addiction ok?)

The brain is a huge energy suck, and the cortex is the biggest pig of all.

The brain's survival parts, by design, use very little electricity, very little energy.

We use the most energy when making new plans, designing projects, and putting together new combinations of thoughts that previously didn't exist. "New" means heating up the ingredients to form freshly baked plans, plays, songs, sculptures, or characters.
The more I understand how my brain works, the more in control of my thoughts, emotions and creativity I'll be!

I'll learn how I work!

Natural light is good for eyes, brain, immune system.

Mr. Bee says, "Listening, feeling, seeing, using awareness to combine things in new ways. This is art."

Artists, the
pre-frontal cortex
is where the
action happens,
the "pfc" is
where we create.

Princess Amygdala

October 3 11:34 pm

Steven told me he's bringing an old girlfriend to the play with us. I told him that'd be fine... I hate her. What's he doing with her on our date? I can't even think straight. Arghhh!!!!!!!

This is what Bee said happens...I get it. My amygdala, the emotions taking over... I can't write anymore...I'm too upset. Amy, her name is Amy. She's 26 and a flight attendant. Probably gorgeous!!!!!! I'm sure she has breasts. He's mine. This isn't fair. He bought me a sandwich. He loves me and only me!

Uggh!

October 3 12:01 midnight

He didn't even ask me if she could come. He just dropped this bomb on me. "Amy's coming with us to Alec's play!" Like I have no feelings? Like it's not an issue!! I'm not going. Forget them.

And...

October 3 12:21 am

I don't want to miss the play. I'm the little kid he's hanging out with while he's all into her curvy, womanly ways. That's stupid. I'm not going. Alec deserves better friends than that. How can he just tell me about Amy now?   Sorry...this is bad blogging.

On to the Play

October 3 12:42 am

I asked Ginger to come with me to the play. Alec's my friend and Ginger needs a friend right now, too. Her band split up, creative differences, whatever. Steven's a jerk.

My mammal Parts

October 4   10:52 pm

Last night I re-read the chapter and lecture about the adrenaline meter after my adrenaline meter went off the scale. I can't believe I sent out that blog when I was in such a ramped up emotional state. Thank god I have a readership of my English teacher and Alec.

I lost my mind. I went fully into my mammalian brain where my emotions shut down my human brain.

The cortex gets fueled only when the other parts are satisfied.

The PFC pulls energy into it when it can, when we allow it. Chaos fueled my mammal parts, not my human parts last night.

In my tantrum, I felt no subtlety and had no focus. I was out of my creative mind.

Thank you Mr. Bee for letting me know what goes on even when I'm out of my mind. I got back to sane quicker, just because I could see what was going on.

The cortex gets fueled only when the other parts are satisfied.

ADRENALINE METER

ADRENALINE METER

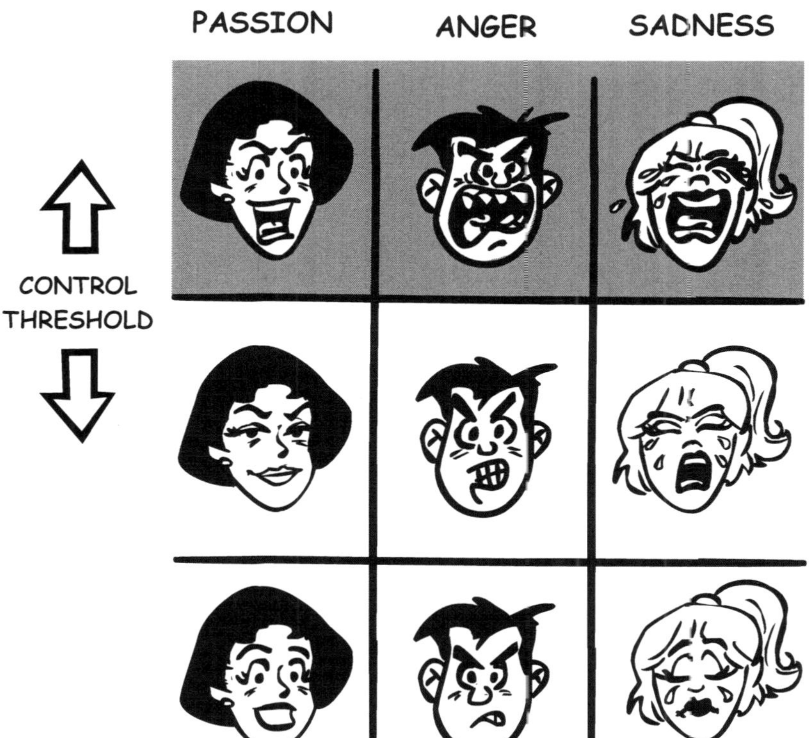

Black Swan

Our stage can bring in old thoughts, new thoughts, colors, costumes or anything we want. The challenge is that we have limited space and time for auditions, rehearsals and performances. We can only have so many actors on the stage at one time or it becomes like a manic-monkey zoo exhibit.

I saw the movie "Black Swan" and I just can't get it out of my head. The dark side of this ballerina resonates with my greatest fears and she keeps coming into my head. I love her and feel so much like her sometimes. Maybe if I draw her I can go on with my other work.

The optimum number of thoughts to bring on stage at once is between two and seven.

Most of us do well to explore and combine two or three thoughts at a time. By working the stage often, we get better at it and raise our abilities.

Thinking is a skill just like pot making or playing an instrument.

Creating is innate, yet we can learn our whole lives how to be better at it.

Bee added, "Because of the artist's ability to prolifically combine different ideas and act them out, artists are rarely role models for any societal norms."

Creating isn't magic, no matter what you've been told.

CREATING is a repeatable behavior.

Creating is a repeatable behavior.

Creating is a repeatable behavior.

Creating is repeatable behavior.   It looks different every time because it's creative.

As an artist, I know that creating and having ideas aren't my main issue.

Keeping the wannabe "other thoughts" off the stage is my biggest challenge.

When I'm working on pots, my mind can wander off. Spending any brain power imagining a drawing of a brain or the amoeba I drew in ninth grade can distract me from the experience of pot making. Focusing on just the texture, water, and pressure of the pot are three things right there. Any more thoughts on stage and I miss the moment of learning, the creative moment.

Focusing on keeping other actors, even fine actors, off stage when it's not their scene is crucial to the creative process.

Allowing actors to appear only in the scenes I want is a required practice and discipline of the creative mind.

The director, which is me, my "Self," controls my mind.

No outside forces control my mind.

The Self – this is who I am. The SELF is the creative director of my inner world.

My Self controls my stage. My Self, the director, has done a nice job on this entry. Steven is an actor who kept trying to jump into this blog. I've kept him off my stage for this whole journal entry. He's not relevant to this blog. Now, I can't stop thinking about him.

He's back, stomping on my heart. I'll return to blogging when he's off my stage.

Thinking is a skill just like pot making or playing an instrument.

Excellence Exercise:

List five times when your focus was good.

1. _______________________________

2. _______________________________

3. _______________________________

4. _______________________________

5. _______________________________

Alec

Alec tried to kill himself his senior year. Kind of. He gave me the okay to write about it. He didn't take enough pills to do the deed, but checked himself into the psych ward anyway.

Being artistic made him feel different his whole life. His sexuality was only a small part of his feeling of isolation, the grief he got from other kids, and the lack of support from adults in his life. He saw the world very differently than others around him, and he dared to express himself honestly.

He was mocked, bullied and ostracized. Teachers and other adults often supported his mainstream-thinking tormentors who at church, school, and on the playground. He dared to question and got beaten down for his creative thinking and lifestyle.

The way he thought kept him alone. As he saw it, he was weird and unaccepted, unacceptable as a person.

With macho, fixed-mindset father and brothers, and a depressed, drunken mother who denied her own artistic passions, Alec saw no future in his family. Worse, he saw no people in the world around him with whom he could relate. He survived with a strong Self once he found that Self. He learned to quiet his mind with help from a friend at the hospital.

Alec knew about his adrenaline meter and the destructive loops he was in mentally.

Depression and isolation are common amongst artists. That's why Bee took the time to talk about it.

Bee told us a story about medicating our sadness and depression. He calls it the "Negative Highway" story.

J's Lecture No.6

The Negative Highway

Most creatives I know have suffered from one form of depression or another in their lives. I have even heard some creatives say that they do their best work when they are feeling down or moody. That may be true, but staying in a depressed state can have lasting physical and emotional consequences.

I'm going to go out on a limb and say we primarily live in a negative culture. The media bombards us with negative news and all the things going wrong in the world, including the end of the world. I think more people criticize than give praise. I have noticed in my students that most of their inner dialogue is negative.

To show my students how their brain works, I usually draw a rough sketch of a brain cell or neuron and go through the functions of the various parts. Then I explain that when you have a thought, the cells link together to create a strand or neural network. The more you repeat the thought, the stronger the neural connection becomes. Add in some adrenaline and you've got a thought that will likely be stored in your long-term memory.

I then use the analogy of building a highway. The first time you have a thought, it is like walking through a field or forest. If you only walk that way once, it will probably go unnoticed, but if you continue to travel that path again and again, a trail will develop. Travel it more and your brain will see the need to build a road. As your traffic grows, so will your road, until you have a multi-lane highway complete with outdoor advertising and access roads. This highway can either be a positive or negative highway.

If your thinking is primarily negative, your highway will be negative. Your billboards might have sayings like "You are ugly" or "You suck at relationships." Eventually, these continuous negative thoughts will manifest themselves into negative results and then depression. Remember, THOUGHT = BEHAVIORS = RESULTS.

If the results become severe, people need to seek the advice of a professional. Often in our "quick cure" culture, some type of medication is prescribed. Medicating depression, to continue our analogy, is essentially getting off the highway and driving on the access road parallel to the highway. Eventually life will throw its inevitable curve balls and right back on to the highway you will go, only to be prescribed a higher dose of the medication.

Don't get me wrong. I am not entirely against medication. I see it as a tool. However, the problem remains that instead of working on building a positive highway to get back on track and take life in a new direction, most people don't exert the effort. They choose instead to ride on the access road until the next bump puts them back on the negative highway they have spent years developing.

So what is the solution? How can I build a positive highway and leave depression behind me? To illustrate this point, I borrow an example from renowned psychologist, Dr. Sigmund Freud. Freud felt that the human mind was like an iceberg sitting in an ocean. The top of the iceberg is our conscious mind and is much smaller in proportion to the massive subconscious below the water.

I believe our conscious mind is limited, and many thoughts lie beneath our awareness. No one would choose to be unhappy on purpose. All your results, experiences and life events cause you to view information and people through the colored lenses of your unconscious mind. Some of these perceptions may be "True," while others may be "False." The point is that we make decisions based on our impressions and limited childhood perception and then stick to these decisions without true awareness as to why.

Our unconscious minds keep the code books. The more conscious we become, the more aware we are of our mind's power and the origins of some of these negative pathways.

NEGATIVE HIGHWAY

Our filters change as we age. Through your conscious thoughts, for example, if you say to yourself, in a moment of despair, "I am horrible at relationships," this imprints into your unconscious mind for later viewing. Your conscious mind may only partially believe this to be true, but your unconscious mind will accept this as fact. The reverse is also true. If you tell yourself, "I am an amazing artist." Your conscious mind may perceive this to be false, however your unconscious mind essentially says, "Oh wow!!! I am an amazing artist."

This is how you create your positive highway – by gaining more awareness of your highways, and telling yourself the positive ideas you want to be true about yourself, even if you don't initially believe them. Your conscious mind might initially reject these thoughts and feed the seeds of doubt. Remember, THOUGHTS = BEHAVIORS = RESULTS. Positive thoughts on a continued basis will direct your mind and body towards positive behaviors, which will eventually manifest into positive results.

Many of you may be reading this and thinking, "you can't just think your way out of depression" and that this is just more of the endless barrage of feel good "pop psychology" dribble. Having used these techniques to bring myself out of severe depression in my twenties, I can tell you it works. And I did it without the assistance of medication. I will end this lecture the way I sometimes deal with particularly bright students who challenge me on my statements from time to time with a Dr. Phil style answer, "If you have all the right answers and know so much, you must be getting the results you want, right?"

Negating Highway Exercise:

List five negative thoughts that might be ho ding you
back in any part of your life.

1. ____

2. ____

3. ____

4. ____

5. ____
(You don't have to share these with anyone.)

Rather than take drugs to get by, and not deal with his issues, Alec
found another way to change his inner chemicals.

A nurse on his floor taught him to quiet his mind through a non-
religious meditation. The brain reacts to stimulation in certain ways.
Stimulation increases our respiration and heart rate. The chemicals we
manufacture change our body chemistry towards or away from the four
f's: fighting, fleeing, feeding, or finding a mate.

Mammal reactions are not actions initiated by our human intelligence, but
reactions to outer stimulation without conscious thought. Like lab rats.

B.F. Skinner studied rats to predict human behavior because
emotionally, we're very similar to rats.

Creative thinking happens when we use the human parts of our brain,
not the lower functions.

Meditating quiets our mammal parts and allows the human Self to take
control of our lives.

PUSH FOR PLEASURE

Mammal
reactions are not
actions initiated
by our human
intelligence,
but reactions to
outer stimulation
without conscious
thought.
Like lab rats.

Meditating saved Alec's life.

Quieting the beast is only one by-product of meditating.

Emotions are reactions.

We absolutely need to run from the tiger or jump out of the way of a car, so reacting can be great... just not as often as the fear mongers on the FearNews would have us react.

I argued that I want to put emotions into my art, not separate myself from my feelings.

Bee agreed about emotions and put it another way:

"Feelings are vital in creation, yet conscious awareness of feelings is what makes it art, and not feces smeared on the wall."

I let go of my anger, my mammal response. Steven is Steven and in control of his life, his journey. I have my journey. I like him. Stop it... let it go. Thoughts are just thoughts and they don't define me.

Bee suggested we form an artist group to meet socially for play, talk, and idea sharing on any topic from our art to business to relationships.

Isolation in our creativity is often necessary, but not when away from work.

"Feelings are vital in creation, yet conscious awareness of feelings is what makes it art, and not feces smeared on the wall."

Sugar Rush

October 7 12:39 am

My ass is growing. Easy on the cupcakes...I sit and read and draw. I get so hungry. I'm going for a walk after I eat my sweets.

An enjoyable state of flow is not limited to artists. Plumbers, surgeons, mechanics, and just about any skilled activity can engage our human brain so actively that we feel happy.

The state of happiness is often the "state of flow." Immersion into a project creates a physical/mental state where we feel good.

Our brain chemicals, generated by activity or inactivity, control our mood.

Bee wants us to be happy artists, not artists who suffer most of the time. All artists suffer sometimes.

He told us a story:

Thomas Edison used to think about a problem, then close his eyes while lying on a bench holding weights in each hand. As soon as he drifted off to sleep, he'd drop the weights and wake up from the loud thud. He used this light-sleep state as a creative state of consciousness and would often have a good answer when he awoke. He quieted his mind to allow the answer to bubble up from the depths.

I, too, wake up sometimes with a fresh idea, especially when I go to bed thinking about it.

I'm now keeping a pad and pen by my bed for Edison moments. Napolean Hill wrote about this state of almost asleep in THINK and GROW RICH. As if I'll ever be rich? But, maybe.

Eat to Live

I skipped ahead a few chapters in BRILLIANCE to "fuel for the brain." It takes more energy to think creatively than to go with a routine. This explains why the more I sit, draw, study, and engage my brain, the more I want to eat. We evolved as a specie, and we survived by thinking on the go. Our bodies are similar to our ancestors' bodies that wandered the plains, gathered nuts and berries, and hunted.

I throw like a girl or a very weak boy. I'm certain my great, great, great aunts survived gathering berries and not by throwing spears at saber-tooth tigers.

Humans thought on the go, created while on the move. Sitting and learning for long stretches of time isn't natural for our bodies or brains.

Physically and emotionally, we've evolved very little in the previous 20,000 years.

Our biology is very similar to our close ancestors, those wanderers and hunters. By contrast, our thoughts have changed dramatically from viral memes passed through technology, radio, television, internet, twitter...

Intellectually, we've had huge evolutions evidenced by tools and technology.

Thought evolutions occur much, much faster than gene changes. Memes spread quickly.

As a kid, my dad had no computer, cell phone, email, twitter, or running water. They had to poop in a hole in the ground called an "outhouse." They lived in the rural parts and grew their own vegetables. No wonder he's so all over me about getting a REAL job. I can't grow my own food and he's afraid I'll live with him and my nine cats for the rest of my life. I don't even have a cat, so what's he all worried about? It would be awesome fun to have a kitten. Maybe I should get a cat?

Oxygen and glucose are the fuel for our brains and bodies. The stage, upon which we create, uses the most energy of any part of our body or brain. That's why we're hungry when we learn and create.

Oxygen is a huge part of the brain-fuel equation.

Glucose is the sugar we break food down into, and use as fuel. The sugar we crave can be supplied by Jolt Cola, Doritos, and cupcakes. Those "quick carbs" fuel us for a short amount of time. The "longer carbs," like whole grains and nuts, last longer for fuel, as does protein. Nuts and berries that I gathered on the plains are healthier, less ass-growing foods.

Like a carburetor (Dad fixes his car), the right mixture of oxygen and fuel make for a better running engine.

Oxygen and food in our bodies perform similar functions, so when we get less oxygen, we crave more food.

Exercise...I know, exercise makes for better energy when we have the glucose in the right amounts too. Now that Ginger has quit drugs for the third time, she wants to start running. Running? Let's try walking first. Habits, at least it might be a better habit.

Oxygen and food in our bodies perform similar functions, so when we get less oxygen, we crave more food.

EXERCISE is HUGELY important for healthy brain function and creativity.

More sugar alone will eventually just make me sleepy from the insulin production that manages and regulates sugar flow to my cells.

(...and unwanted belly and ass fat.)

Science was so boring. Now it's relevant. I can be a better artist, and more creative, the better I feed my brain the right mix of fuel.

I now care about science realizing that I'm my own science fair project.

EXERCISE is hugely important for healthy brain function and creativity.

Cup o' Joe

October 11 1:59 am

Dad smiled when I brought him a coffee mug that I made in pottery class. I wrote on his mug, "BEST DAD EVER." Dad has every right to worry about me. It was great to make him smile though. I'm his artist daughter, the soon to be eccentric cat lady who lives with him in our fur inundated house.

Ms. Keats told us today, "Take time before you share what you create. Give yourself an insulation period which gives you more time to shed the vulnerability you feel upon giving birth to the idea. It needs to breathe as much as you need the time to better understand it." Imagine if I showed my first pots to Dad. From his special-ed cat-lady.

Flow

October 12 1:43 am

Alec was wonderful in his performance. He just disappeared into the role and became that man he was portraying. He calls it a state of flow. Not coincidentally, the book FLOW is in my Brilliance class. An Austrian guy, Mihaly Csikszentmihalyi, studied happy people and coined the phrase "Flow," as a "state of being" where time ceases to exist and we're totally focused on the task at hand. We're happy in the state of flow, without worries about things not in that moment. I'm happy not trying to pronounce his name out loud.

As Alec described his stage experience, it reminded me of being a little kid everyday, when I didn't know the time or the day and drew pictures and played games with my friends. These days, I only sometimes feel flow, mainly when I draw. Steven talks about how when he writes he disappears into his characters.

By controlling our stage, our inner world where we create, we enter a heightened state of being, human thinking.

Working on a project requires control of our easel, stage, or practice room, both inner and outer control.

Unwanted actors, cell phones, cleaning crews, and audience members have no place on stage during rehearsals or performance.

A strong director keeps distracting thoughts off the stage, allowing us to enter the state of flow.

Bee and Keats must have a conspiracy. They say the same things.

Director Exercise:

Who are the biggest clowns trying to get onto your stage uninvited? Name four distracting thoughts.

1. ____

2. ____

3. ____

4. ____

By controlling our stage, our inner world where we create, we enter a heightened state of being, human thinking.

Candy

Just came back from a 1.7 mile walk.   From another BRILLIANCE textbook: Brain Rules, by John J. Medina, he says,

"Exercise is cognitive candy.   We need to move."

We survived as a specie, not by becoming stronger or developing bigger fangs, but by being smarter.   We create bigger neural networks when we exercise our bodies and brains. We have more energy to carry more information by working and raising our oxygen intake. We create more capillaries for carrying food and nutrients to cells, and de-tox our cells better with exercise. Cells poop, too. Clear out the poop.

The actions of the PFC (our stage) are:
>   (1) problem solving,
>   (2) maintaining attention, and
>   (3) inhibiting emotional impulses.

Our developed cortex is what separates us from animals and teenagers.

We can survive without food for 30 days.

We can survive without water for 7 days.

We can survive without oxygen for 5 minutes.

Ergo, oxygen is the most important intake, ever.

(I've always wanted to writer "ergo".)

I can survive without chocolate for 48 hours.

Oxygen fuels and de-toxes the brain.

"Exercise is cognitive candy. We need to move."

Exercise Exercise:

Name five forms of exercise you might enjoy, or like to try.

1. ____

2. ____

3. ____

4. ____

5. ____

Exercise also regulates the 60+ known neurotransmitters.

Bee's hormone lecture came with a big disclaimer that this is simplified information and not what's taught to doctors and pharmacists.

Three of the most important neurotransmitters, the chemicals that run our brain, are serotonin, dopamine, and nor-epinephrine.

Let's make them three goddesses: Sera, Dopa, and Nora.

Exercise also regulates the 60+ known neurotransmitters.

I never want to spell those words again...Just found out today that Bee doesn't take off for spelling errors so long as he understands that we know what we're talking about. This is an art class, a creative class, so creative spelling is acceptable. Yeaaaaaaaaa!!! Still, I'm not even trying to spell a few names though. The flow guy, forget it!

Ms. Keats is also forgiving on spelling and grammar so long as we write everyday. Taking the fear out makes writing more fun too.

The optimum state of arousal for our stage is created by having a good mix of Dopa and Nora.

Nora is like adrenaline for the brain.

Nora gives us alertness when something's happening and we need to pay attention. When we have sufficient Nora, we're alert and on guard.

NORA feeds the fear in us.

When the tall grasses move as we walk, is it a tiger? We stay alert for opportunities and danger by producing Nora. We might see a tree with berries or dark chocolate kisses?

Unlike Nora, Dopa likes fresh new things. Dopa is happy juice for the brain.

Dopa feeds the happiness in us.

Unexpected events, novelty, punch-lines and discovery stimulate the manufacture of this feel-good juice, Dopa.

We can even produce dopa by thinking about fun things ahead. (optimism)

When I was sick as a kid, my dad would tell me to think of my favorite place. He had no clue that dopa was produced, but he knew my mind could take me to a better mental place and that would make me feel better.

Say "yes" to Dopa.

Little kids are dopa factories because everything is new and fresh. No wonder kids are so happy. Dirt is new.

When we're alert (Nora) and excited about fun new things (Dopa), we have the perfect environment to create on stage.

Unexpected events, novelty, punch-lines and discovery stimulate the manufacture of this feel-good juice, Dopa.

Our best teachers use humor to teach.

Humor creates the feel-good Dopa.

We're more open to learning and storing new info when it feels fresh. The new info is attached to fun-ness and we make chemicals that enjoy the fresh approach, so we want more. I've got to admit, it feels good in Bee's class, now. It's fun to see the world new. I feel better after a day of BRILLIANCE.

Sera regulates emotions and mood, as the chemical police. The pharmaceuticals, Xanex and Prozac, assist Sera in controlling our emotions. I prefer to figure it out internally, rather than buy drugs, but they seem to help Mrs. Chaney next door. I think a divorce from that control-freak, ogre, Mr. Chaney would help her more, but she didn't ask me. She asked her doctor.

Our best teachers use humor to teach.

Only with regulation of emotions will we get a stage with the focused actors we want. Distraction is way too easy for a creative mind.

We all have committees and random thoughts trying to get onto our stage. Debbie Downer, streakers, movie talkers, Animal House frat boys, Freddie Kruger, Madonna, rock singers without boundaries just to name a few. Add guilty inner anima, angry animus, or alien mother ... and anyone else not invited to our rehearsal or creative session, we need Sera.

Sera minds the zoo. Sera's the park ranger, the theatre usher, the bouncer. This neuro-chemical allows the performers to play on stage while she keeps the drunks and loud talkers in line.

Party!

October 15 12:45 am

Speaking of which, I'm going to a party with Gingo and Alec. When Ginger saw Alec on stage she was in awe of his commitment. He loves her boldness and wants to go shopping with us and dress her. I have two girlfriends!!

Fear raises adrenaline, the brain's Nora, so attention is raised too.

The problem with raised Nora is a negative expectation, which in turn lowers the Dopa. Not good for the creative stage.

Fear might keep drunks off the stage, but it also likely scares the musicians to the point they forget their chords and lyrics. Creative work must be fun to be at its best. Dopa is the fun chemical.

Managers of creatives would be wise to know this about fear:

Fear paralyzes the actors and closes down their process.

Fear doesn't work for your creative team, period.

Bee got really hopped-up about this today in class. Although he's a free-lance artist, his main source of income is corporate animation.

He teaches because he loves artists. He wrote this book and designed this course from his love of creative thinking. During this lecture, Bee's amygdala, the emotional part of his brain, got really activated when he talked about sometimes managing projects with fixed-thinking, fear-driving corporate-types. He turned red in the face.

His adrenaline rose noticeably. When I called him on his emotional shift during the lecture, he paused, and then he laughed with humble recognition and gave me this huge smile. He said he'd hug me but the school policy forbids touching. Even in Brilliance you can't hug!? How dumb is that?

Then Bee took a couple of deep breaths and paused. Noticeably more relaxed, he got very serious when he talked about working in the real world as an artist. Keeping yourself in a strong creative mind frame is a big part of being a professional and why so few make it in art as a business.

Art's a job – a fun job – but you've got to manage your brain juices to create every day.

Being able to re-create your brain stage consciously and repeatedly is your job.

Creative thinking is not some mystical state your Dad doesn't understand. It requires discipline, and involves science and high consciousness.

Fear paralyzes the actors and closes down their process. Fear doesn't work for your creative team, period.

Creation is the hardest job a brain can do... it's why so few people have the stamina to create over and over again.

Learning how to be creative over and over, every day is too challenging for many, and why so many amateur artists love creation, yet remain amateurs. It's fun, yet it's really hard. Doing it every day and getting paid for your creativity, you've got to really figure yourself out.

It takes knowing your brain, skills, weaknesses, health, having nurturing supportive relationships, getting enough exercise, a good diet, and still have enough energy to put it into... work that someone will pay for.

Mr. Fine asked us, "Does your work move people one way or another?" "2% of all artists are professional enough to make a living at it."

Being able to re-create your brain stage consciously and repeatedly is your job.

"2%
of all
artists are
professional
enough to
make a living
at it."

J's Lecture No.7

The Fear Speech

I attended a conference in which Gary Vaynerchuck, the author of, The Thank You Economy, spoke. Gary built up his father's wine store to over a $65 million business. After his fantastic talk, everyone in the audience got one of his books. I stood in line to get his autograph and while he was signing my book I asked him, "What do you see as the biggest reason why talented and intelligent people don't move to the next level of success?" He looked up at me as if to see if I was serious about the question and said, "Do you really want to know?" I nodded, and he replied, "Fear!"

I have been giving one version or another of "The Fear Speech" to my students since I first started teaching. I noticed that my students were often having great fears that were preventing them from doing the projects I assigned. For some, it was the fear that their skills weren't good enough. For others, it was fear of the software. It seemed that they imagined pushing the wrong button would somehow cause the computer to blow up. Some students just couldn't think of anything "creative" to do.

The useful biological function of FEAR is self-preservation. On the opposite side of the equation is DESIRE. FEAR tends to constrict and paralyze us. DESIRE leads us to take action. If you are truly stretching yourself as a creative, FEAR will never really go away. Through repetition (PRACTICE, PRACTICE, PRACTICE), we become comfortable with particular skills we have learned. What professionals learn to do, when confronted with a particularly difficult challenge, is build on previous results and use DESIRE to work through the fear to take action anyway.

The best way to overcome fear, as the Nike slogan has told us for years, is to "Just Do It!" The act of "getting started" creates momentum. Once you get started, the next step will present itself to you. As you start to see results, DESIRE builds and you take more and more action until you get results. We'll elaborate more in J's "Crap speech." Some of your results will not be what you want. So what? Did you die? You took chances and lived.

One of the quotes I often say is, "Your greatest strength is your greatest weakness." I believe one of the greatest strengths creatives have is a very vivid imagination. Creatives tend to be able to visualize the results they want in incredible detail. If you read any book on goal setting, they will almost certainly talk about visualization as an initial and important part of achieving success.

Unfortunately, many of the students I know use this amazingly powerful vivid imagination to think more about "what can go wrong" instead of "what can go right." They work up in their mind all the possible negative results or all the bad things that can happen and imagine these scenarios in vivid painful detail. Often, the result of this thinking is that in order to avoid anything bad happening, they do nothing or stick to doing what they already know. The really intelligent students that haven't produced results in my classes often find excuses, rationalize, justify or blame others as to why they weren't able to achieve the results they wanted.

I attended another conference where one of the speakers used a pendulum when he was talking about people's comfort zones. The right of center represented risks. The left of center represented rewards. People's comfort zones were shown as lines drawn on the sides of the pendulum, depending on how far to the left and right people were willing to let the pendulum swing. People who were risk averse would only allow their pendulum to swing a little to the right.

It is my opinion that to really succeed as a creative, you need to expand your comfort zone as far as you can. The more you risk, the greater the reward. Life will have ups and downs. When you get knocked down, get right back up. Sure, people might notice, but over time those same people will admire and respect you for doing it again and again.

Once the artist develops mastery, she still has to perform the art. She's never done. Her next piece is the only one she can control. Her next scene, next drawing, next song, next performance keeps her in the moment, the flow...oh my...am I still writing? I must've gotten into flow writing......good night.

One more thing...I want to be a professional artist. I know my brilliant, repeatable creative mindset is the only sure way of becoming a working artist. Luck is fleeting. Connections are nice, yet,

Knowing myself is the only sure way to become an artist.

Good night, again.

I Love Mr. Bee

October 19 1:20 am

Bee's all about us becoming professional artists if that's what we want. He's driven to help us. I love this man. Either way, pros or amateurs, he'll help us all be more creative, and that's fine with him too.

Loosely quoting Bee:

"Even if you have the stamina and commitment it takes to be an artist, managing your career is greatly related to your understanding, not only of yourself, but also of the humans you work with..."

"Clients haven't read Brilliance or taken the class. They don't care about your process, diet, or neuro-transmitters. They want the product of your creative brain, the fruits of your skill set. They want a finished piece, in the timeframe you negotiated, period."

"How you manage people is an art. Managing is not the same as manipulating. Their journey is their own. Each person is motivated for their own purposes, not your purposes. Make your life easier."

"Listen to what they tell you about themselves. They'll tell you everything you need to know about how to work with them if you listen and communicate honestly throughout."

What're their motivations?

What rules do they play by?

Establish what you'll do and not do in a friendly way, in a way they'll understand.

Look at the client's focus, hear their choice of words and the language they speak, and respond in kind. You must develop the flexibility to go there.

J's Lecture No.8

Personality Types

I've always wondered why people do what they do. The Nature vs. Nurture argument questions how much is related to genetics and how much is caused by environment. You don't have to be a scientist to realize the real answer is that both the temperament you are born with and the environment you experience have an impact on what make you,…well YOU!

I spent years reading as many Personality Type books that I could get my hands on and developed my own concept on some basic personality types and the attributes associated with them. The following is not a comprehensive "end-all/ be-all" of personality assessments, but more of a general tool to be used to help you understand yourself and others better.

I believe there are four general personality types: A, B, C, D. Each one has one primary motivation.

A: Achievers – Achievement is their primary goal. They often value themselves and others based on the amount of achievements and success each has enjoyed.

B: "Be Happy" – Happiness is their primary motivation. They spend their lives looking for the things, skills, jobs or people that they think will make them happy.

C: Caretakers – Being needed is the purpose of their existence. The more people that need them, the better.

D: Detail-Oriented – Details and knowledge are what they desire. They put extremely high value on knowledge and respect folks who pay attention to the details in life.

Everyone intuitively knows people are more complex than just these four basic descriptions. So, my model takes into account that people have a Primary and Secondary personality type.

The Primary personality type is closely related to your genetics. It's who you are, instinctively. It's the basic temperament you were born with. The Secondary personality type is what you desire to be more like.

It's important to note that most people have aspects of all the motivations as parts of their personality. However, it is my belief that the Primary and Secondary motivations occupy the majority of our thoughts that enter into the equation, THOUGHTS = BEHAVIORS = RESULTS. What you think about most of the time affects your behaviors and determines your results.

I also believe our emotional health affects our behaviors in relation to our Primary and Secondary personality types. When it comes to mental health, I believe people can be defined as Healthy, Average or Unhealthy. I also believe our mental health can fluctuate on a day-to-day basis depending on what's going on in our lives. (See Boat Speech)

Below is a list of negative behaviors I have observed associated with the four Personality Types. The more unhealthy a person is, the more pronounced the behaviors will be.

<u>Personality</u>	<u>Unhealthy Negative Behaviors</u>
A	Vindictive, Aggressive, Manipulative, Violent
B	Passive Aggressive, Withdrawn, Sad, Lazy
C	Needy, Obsessive, Overbearing, Intrusive
D	Anti-social, Angry, Rude, Violent

*NOTE: Another observation I have noticed is, the more unhealthy people become, they tend to become more self-centered and selfish.

How do I use this information?

If you can figure out the Primary personality type of a person,
you can adjust your style of communication with them to take
into consideration their primary motivations. A's want to make
sure that projects are set up to help them achieve some goal or
recognition. If they are of average or unhealthy mental health,
you can expect some of the unhealthy negative behaviors to
present themselves, especially during stressful times. FEAR is one
of the biggest catalysts for unhealthy negative behaviors to arise.

The main point of this lecture is that people are motivated
differently. Seek to understand who you're dealing with as well
as what the task is. You'll be more successful, have more fun,
develop a better relationship, and give them exactly what they
want.

PERSONALITY TYPES

TYPE	MOTIVATION
A: "Anal-Retentive"	ACHIEVEMENT
B: "Be Happy"	HAPPINESS
C: "Caretaker"	BEING NEEDED
D: "Detail-Orientated"	KNOWLEDGE

The client doesn't need to speak your language or understand you. It's your job to understand what they want and give it to them.

Drawing well isn't enough. Who're you drawing for?

You create for the client in commercial work, for the gallery when you're famous.

When the galleries call you, then do your own thing. Until then, you work with clients.

OMG Moment!

When Bee went into this lecture, an older woman, at least 40, got into it with Bee. Man, Bee gets fired up about this!

Her name is Claire, and she argued with Bee about creating only for yourself, your vision, your sense of what good art is. He flat out told her she must have a rich husband. She stood up, turned red as a beet and told him he was a sell-out, a capitalist and the furthest thing from a real artist. He calmed himself and Claire down, then was amazing with her.

Bee talked about the olden days, when the church, the state, or a wealthy benefactor commissioned artists to do works. The artist had little say. Mostly the vision of the employer was carried out. Galleries and private collectors today keep a few hundred artists alive. 99% of young and old artists have to earn their way in the world and work in offices or free-lance from home.

Then Bee asked, why do you think so many old masterpieces were of ugly people? Answer: Because they had money for a portrait.

Even the gallery-type fine artist works for people. They often create commissioned pieces to match office, garden, or home color schemes, materials, and shapes. Working with and listening to other people is still a skill artists need to have. Who could disagree?

Artists were dependent upon the rich benefactors and mostly the church for employment.

So after we a painta the walls,
we can a painta the ceiling.

The client doesn't need to speak your language or understand you. It's your job to understand what they want and give it to them.

I Love Drawing

I stayed up too late last night drawing.

"How do you get good at something?"

"PRACTICE, PRACTICE, PRACTICE,

RESEARCH, RESEARCH, RESEARCH."

I love drawing. Time flew by. "Flew" and "flow" are related, I'm sure.
I showed Mr. Bee my blog, selective parts, no Steven. He wants me
to intern next semester when I take his animation class. That's one of
the coolest things ever. A professional likes my work and wants me to
intern. He's still a big man with a huge voice, but he doesn't scare or
intimidate me anymore. He's a real artist.

The Beatles played 10,000 hours in the clubs of Hamburg and Liverpool
before they took the U.S. by storm. They mastered their craft. Bill
Gates spent 10,000 hours on the computer from high school until he
started Microsoft. (from Outliers by Malcolm Gladwell.)

It takes 10,000 hours of work to master a skill.

Time invested is the only way towards mastery, yet, still no guarantee of
success.

Thank God I love drawing. It's the best time I ever get to spend, so why
not?

The seeds of the Flow experience, as defined by Dr. Mihaly
Csikszentmihalyi (from now on "Dr. Flow"), came from his childhood
fascination with how dumb adults could behave. As a boy he saw first-
hand the 20th century, European holocaust. Even as a boy, he knew
there was a better way of thinking than whatever led to such stupid,
mean behavior.

The main premise of Brilliance is thoughts dictate actions, which form
our results. Smart in, smart out...or...garbage in, garbage out.

Bee starts every class by writing on the board:

"Thoughts = Actions = Results"

What we think dictates our actions.

To see how productive our thoughts and actions are, we merely need to look at our results. To change our results, we have to change our thoughts first.

How we think creates our art, our life, and our relationships.

Characteristics of the Flow Experience:
1) Clarity of Goal
2) Clarity of feedback
3) Challenge of activity matches well with the person's ability
4) Feeling of focus
5) Effortless
6) Feeling of being in control of your life
7) Lose sense of self-consciousness
8) Sense of time transformed

Being in FLOW is fun and enjoyable and comes when we face new challenges and use skills, whether still developing or honed. We have a sense of timelessness, ego-less-ness, living in the moment with our senses alive and responding...

Flow, flow, flow your boat, gently down the stream...merrily, merrily, merrily, merrily, life is but a dream.

Characteristics of the Flow Experience

1) Clarity of Goal

2) Clarity of feedback

3) Challenge of activity matches well with the person's ability

4) Feeling of focus

5) Effortless

6) Feeling of being in control of your life

7) Lose sense of self-consciousness

8) Sense of time transformed

PART III

Change is Good

October 24 1:12 am

Bee's lecture today:

Depression and the artist. The high feeling of newness and discovery that creative people get to feel is why we do it. By being a mental pioneer, one hitch-hiker on Discovery Road is depression. Not constant, not even predictable, but from time to time we enter an energy lull where we feel stuck or lost.

This lack of connectedness, this off-balance feeling, is because we're constantly taking our world apart and putting it back together in different ways. Our experiments create what's "New in the World."

Less creative people live in a fixed world that creates neither the highs nor the lows we seem to need. They're grounded in their beliefs and status. We're neither grounded, nor concerned with status. We live in flux.

If you choose to embrace the creative lifestyle, your life will have changes in style, process, emotions, friendships, and can feel like paradise in the flow process of work, yet, of course, not always.

Being a professional artist is hard work, and a choice. Finding solid connected parts help immensely. Friendship with other artists and non-artists, good work habits, good loving, hugs, exercise, diet, meditation, and sleep will be huge factors in shortening your depression and maximizing your joyful creativity.

As you go through depressive phases, feel what you feel. Do not numb this great source of material your wide range of emotions brings to your life and your art. Use all of your emotions and experience. Be aware of it and Use it!

Ms. Keats is filming one of her short screenplays next weekend. First of all, my teacher has a real life outside of school? She has hopes and dreams beyond junior college? Then she asked for volunteers. Steven is the cinematographer (cameraman), and of course my best friend Alec is the star. What fun! Of course I'm in! Doing what, I'm not sure.

Drawing pictures, making marshmallow treats?   ;-)

Closely related, after Bee's depression talk in Brilliance we got into:

Pleasure vs. Happiness

:-D vs :-)

There is a big difference between pleasure and happiness. Anyone can find pleasure by eating ice cream, sticking their hand in a cookie jar, or down their pants. It requires no special skills or learned behaviors. Pleasure is not the same as happiness.

Pleasure is genetic. Things that keep the specie going like food, sex, and safety are genetically pleasurable so that people and animals will survive. Therefore:

Pleasure is evolutionary. :-D

Certain acts feel good so the specie will continue to do them and thus ensure survival.

Pleasure is genetic.

Pleasure/Pain Principle – healthy people move towards things that we think will create pleasure and away from things that cause pain.

Also,

Physical pain is genetic. :-<

We're wired so that we don't stab ourselves or eat bitter plants that might kill us. Pain is an evolutionary adaptation to keep our specie thriving and out of danger. Pain means Stop!!!

The sun feels good, so we go outside and get Vitamin D. We walk because exercise feels good and is healthy for us.

More pleasure doesn't bring more happiness. Pleasure is not the source of happiness.

Happiness comes from activities that challenge us, where we can get better, and disappear into them. Those are the happiness paths.

The Flow guy, the Dalai Lama, and Mr. Bee all talk about the thinking that brings us happiness, a worthy path of developing our skills to become better at what we love doing.

Happiness is cultural and comes from learning and doing. ☺ :-)

Recreational drugs feel good. They bring pleasure by changing our chemicals to the feel good ones.

Drugs are not the path towards happiness, and are actually counter-productive to happiness.

Our brains' natural ability to create the Nora, Sera, and Dopa are weakened by artificial highs. Our skills and processing of thoughts create flow, the happiness state of being.

Happiness comes from activities that challenge us, where we can get better, and disappear into them. Those are the happiness paths.

Happiness is human.

Gingo and I have had this discussion several times over the last few weeks. She seems much less artificially altered, and we walk three times a week now.

Simply Complex

October 27   2:02 am

Developing a complex personality is Dr. Flow's answer for happiness.

Pleasure is simple.

Happiness is complex.

Five C's for Developing Yourself

1) <u>Clarity</u> — have clarity of purpose in life. From moment to moment, do things that give feedback so you can see how you're doing and how you need to adjust.

2) <u>Centering</u> — control of your psychic, mental and emotional energy.

3) <u>Choice</u> — create a varitey of choices. We feel powerful when we choose. Tasks we want to do create more good feelings than those we have to do.

4) <u>Commit Yourself</u> — passion and energy towards something. Care for it, give care to it.

5) <u>Challenge</u> — keep upping the challenge. Look for novelty. New is fun and engaging to try to master.

-The 'Flow' Guy (Mihaly Csikszentmihalyi)

Accomplishment is not a worthy goal. The doing must be why we do it.

Fixed mindsets value only the result.

Growth mindsets value the experience.

French philosopher, Jean-Paul Sartre said, "The greatest gift a father can give his son is to die early...feeling abandoned or left out...they find out earlier how to find enjoyment."   Not sure I agree, but my dad will never read this blog anyway. Point made that we all have to find our happiness by what we enjoy doing.

Boredom and worry are lack of focus...mind going in circles...not using your mind, not efficient, nothing is happening. What we focus on defines the results we get.

Duress challenges the ability to flow...confronting tragedies successfully makes life better.

Having some stress aids our focus, but too much stress wears down our ability to handle it (and our immune system.)

The more we use our bouncers (Sera) to keep actors off the stage, the more tired the bouncers get, and then we need a break.
I'm not sleeping enough lately. It affects my mood and my art. Is re-telling someone else's thoughts creative? Yes, if artfully done through my interpretation.

Halloween

November 1 2:47 am

Alec dressed as a Hooter's waitress, Ginger as a football player, and I was Cleopatra for Halloween. Steven is forgiven. He came to the party as Satan, which diffused my anger, and made me laugh at myself. He's too old for me anyway and likes Amy. We're friends again and had a blast at this haunted house. Amy's actually alright. She wore a nurse's costume that showed off her cleavage, but I'm over the jealousy. Up way too late, exhausted.   Zzzzzzzzzz

Sleeeeepppp

November 2 1:23 am

Sleep is huge. Bee reminds us how important sleep is.

Dolphins sleep in shark-filled waters.

Sleep is so hugely important, dolphins sleep in shifts, propping each other up so they don't drown while acting as look-outs so they don't get eaten by a great white shark.

Dolphins sleep in shark-filled waters.

Sleep is a biological necessity or why would dolphins risk their lives every night, or sheep sleep with wolves on the prowl?

A sleep study on the network TV show, 20/20, documented that sleep-deprived college students turned diabetic in three to five days...those studied showed their appetite gauges were wrecked in three days of inadequate sleep. They didn't know when they were full or hungry. With just three days of disturbed sleep, they became over-eaters. Sleep is important to a creative mind and rear-end girth.

A lab rat died after being kept awake for five days in a row. Our mammal brain is very similar to a rat's brain. That's why it's called the "rat race."

In bed before 2 a.m. from now on... Midnight bed-time by next week?

Down Day

November 3   12:23 am

I'm sad for no apparent reason. Where will I live as an artist? All these lectures about how to live as an artist. I can't do it. I'm folding jeans and living with Mom and Dad, writing this stupid blog, making pots, and studying about how I'm so Brilliant. I don't feel brilliant today.

What can I do to make a living doing what I love, at what makes me happy?

Who'll hire me? Theories are bullshit, I'm tired of trying.

I'm exhausted.

Up Again!

November 3   1:44 am

A glorious nap. I'm brilliant again and gonna draw tonight.

A.C.R.

November 4   12:55 am

"Don't Miss Your Life," by Joe Robinson, is an extra credit reading assignment. He says, "Autonomy, competence, and relatedness are the keys to a happy life.

Choosing to draw (autonomy), especially what I want to draw, being good at it (competence), and having friends (relatedness) – those are the things that make me happy.

Autonomy – Choosing my courses, and to be an artist

Competence – I'm a good illustrator

Relatedness – I have true friends who share and support my values.

So, yea! I do have a life.

Fine said, "Doing art that is accepted develops your tools and gives you a sense of confidence. Learn how it's been done already. These proven methods, angles, and processes allow you to not have to re-invent the wheel."

"As you grow in your field, you can choose to veer away from accepted practices, rejecting what you feel inhibits. When you go into uncharted territory, enter with a proven set of tools."

Mr. Fine quotes from ART AND FEAR a lot.

Tool Exercise:

List five tools you have towards being a professional.

1. ____

2. ____

3. ____

4. ____

5. ____

The Rush

November 5   1:02 am

The combo of brain chemicals puts your brain in a positive mental state by imagining rewards, interactions that are fun, or money from your work. Positive thoughts create a good state to work in, making dopamine even before the events. Positive thoughts change our chemistry.

Children get a chemical rush of interest...it happens in a flash. I can do that.

Humor with positive expectations creates a good internal environment...or "invironment"...cool, I like that...Invironment.

I made up a word: "Invironment"

Bee loved "invironment" and used it in his lecture right away. He talked of nature vs. nurture and how we become who we become.

Bee said, "Our genetics determine which environments we feel comfortable in, so our "invironment" can determine what environments we end up in."

Dopamine results from the positive mindset, a growth mindset, unafraid of results. That's unlike that fixed mindset, buzz-killing way of thinking. That's why "pounds of pots" produces the best pots. This is why having fun and playing is better for artists than harsh grading for pot thickness or design experiments gone awry.

Art teachers and bosses (the good ones) understand dopamine and growth mindset.

Feel good = Work good

I love naps. I'm brilliant after good sleep, and not depressed. Still, 2:20 bedtime needs to change someday.   Less caffeinated dark chocolate...

J's Lecture No.9

The Boat Speech

When I was taking my first psychology courses, I learned about the concept of Locus of Control. There are two loci of control:

Internal Locus of Control – where individuals believe they have some control over their lives.

External Locus of Control – where individuals believe the environment determines their life.

These two perceptions stuck in my mind over the years and I came to think of them as ways in which people either sail through life, or steer their own boat. People with an external locus of control tend to put up their sails and let the wind, or external events, guide them through life. Individuals with an internal locus of control set their sails towards particular destinations.

At a recent seminar, one of the speakers pointed out that we learn in school the shortest distance between two points is a straight line. However, rarely does our life take a linear path. We often look back and see the path we have taken had all sorts of twists and turns. So, whether you choose to be driven by internal or external forces, be prepared for an interesting ride.

I chose to follow the internal locus of control philosophy. I like to feel I have some control over my destination in life, but that doesn't mean I have total control over every aspect. I tell my students that they can't control the weather and should expect some storms. After all, what compelling story about an ocean journey doesn't have at least one great storm sequence? These storms can take the form of car accidents or loss of a person or job. We may then find ourselves floating amongst the debris of our wrecked boat or stranded on a deserted island, hoping that another boat will come by to rescue us.

Most of the time, these situations are temporary. It is normal to grieve and even feel a little sorry for ourselves. However, we have the choice to either just float in the water and hope we don't become dinner for any passing sharks or grab a piece of drift wood, start paddling as fast as we can and hope we find land. The fantastic part of being a human being is we have the ability to adapt to most situations. It is up to you where you wind up in life.

All that Jazz

I'm trying to get to bed earlier. Habits are challenging to break.

Bee talked about over-arousal costing him a job...over-arousal can be as bad as under arousal...When he was young, new to the business and the city, he was so stoked about his presentation that he missed his turn on the way to the meeting, and when he got in front of the client, he was so jazzed about his idea, and overloaded with what he was going to say, he didn't listen. Not listening due to over-arousal cost him that job. He learned that one can be too jazzed.

The optimum creative state is a good mix of arousal and fun, Nora and Dopa.

One way to control your stage is to make lists before you get to the theatre. Plan ahead the elements of that day's work.

Filmmakers study scripts, make lists, and use storyboards before they arrive at the set. Make lists and use them.

One way to control your stage is to make lists before you get to the theatre. Plan ahead the elements of that day's work.

Make lists and use them.

Lists give you control of who's going to be on the stage and when.
What scenes are we running today? Who's in the scene? What will
it look like? Tech rehearsal? Do I need more sienna for my palate?
Which songs are we rehearsing? Interview the choreographer at noon.

I've been storyboarding for Ms. Keats' romantic film about a loving
ghost haunting her still-living husband. I feel a shade kiss-ass helping
my teacher, but it's really fun working on a creative team with my
friends.   : -)   Ms. Keats has a first name and it's Lori.

MAKE LISTS OF IDEAS

Refer to your lists often

Steven, although he's a writer, and not a graphic artist like Bee, does exactly what Bee suggested...He's always with a pen and pad or laptop writing things down in list form instead of carrying around the thoughts in his head and risking losing them.

He keeps lists of plots, jokes, dialogue, and characters he wants to use now, or on a future project.

LIST List:

List seven areas of your life where lists can help.

1. ____

2. ____

3. ____

4. ____

5. ____

6. ____

7. ____

Learning new stuff raises dopa. New brain connections raise dopa. New isn't limited to art stuff. New hobbies, new friends...new is new and stimulates the dopa.

Novelty activates the brain in a fun way...too much novelty scares us, overloads, then nora comes on and we freeze.

That's why work habits, a cozy bed to draw on, or a table we like, or desk with keyboard pads are good...habits can aid in comfort, while we're exploring new things mentally. Creating a safe "invironment" to adventure from...we can control parts of our life.

COMFORT List:

List eight things that help your creative space.

1. _______________________________________

2. _______________________________________

3. _______________________________________

4. _______________________________________

5. _______________________________________

6. _______________________________________

7. _______________________________________

8. _______________________________________

Novelty or sameness? Some of both...happy thoughts, happy thoughts.......more dopa, the art of art, better art through healthier lifestyle.....I'm self-hypnotizing myself.

BRAINWAVES

TYPE		Hz	STATE
GAMMA		30 +	VERY ACTIVE
BETA		12 - 30	ACTIVE

FLOW

ALPHA		8 - 12	RELAXED
THETA		4 - 8	VERY RELAXED
DELTA		0 - 4	DEEP SLEEP

I'm a Grip!

November 7 1:45 am

I helped on *Ghostly Love*, Lori's film.   She must forgive this short entry since I volunteered. My tasks today: I bought Sonic burgers, carried lights, dragged cables, helped mic up the actors, and applied make-up. Physical work is hard. Good night.

SFX

November 8 7:48 am

Did I mention this is a two day shoot. Yesterday, Bee came to the set. He's doing SFX (Special Effects and the graphics) and wants to help any way he can. Bee mentioned the Dalai Lama in passing on set. On the reading list for next semester's BRILLIANCE II class, The Dalai Lama writes about "Mindfulness" – being mindful, knowing your mind. I may even read it ahead of time.

A State of Being

November 9 7:40 pm

With so many artists coming together and from different directions, this weekend on a film set changed my life. Alec was funny and smooth and emotional. Steven was low key, but really present. Lori, the writer-director, was so in charge. English teacher by day, filmmaker by whenever she can, Lori is my new hero. I'll never write for a living, but now I understand her passion for telling a story well.

Bee's class makes more sense and why he's coming at us from so many different directions. I love learning about how I function.   Maybe I have a future as an artist?

Bee started on brain waves and biology.

The Alpha state – most adults sleep through this unless they are in flow or train their minds to be awake in alpha. Kids are often wide awake in alpha. This is a very aware and receptive state of being. It's why kids learn more easily than adults. Edison knew of the alpha state without knowledge of brain waves. His bench naps utilized this very intelligent, open state of being. Alpha is a great problem-solving state.

Beta is a revved up state, excellent for tasks we're already skilled at, but not a receptive state where creative thinking takes place. Beta is the worst listening state. Wait to share sensitive info if your friend is in beta.

Fast beta brain waves make it harder for new thoughts to enter a mind. Calmer is better for learning. Alpha is calmer, more open to new info.

The "insight state" – immediately before we have a brainstorm or breakthrough on an idea, we get a burst of super-fast gamma waves. Then our brains return to alpha. Insights can actually be encouraged and repeated with training.

Theta brain waves indicate a very relaxed state, where only trained monks are conscious. Delta is a baby, deep-sleep state. No one is known to be conscious in this state.

The Task at Hand

November 10 11:56 am

Mindfulness is a flow state where we're aware of more around us, especially as it relates to the task at hand. When we are focused on a task with clarity of the goal, we are mindful. For me, pottery and drawing create mindfulness. I go into flow sometimes driving, where I see ahead, make good decisions, or occasionally while cooking. Two summers ago, when I worked as a health-food short-order cook, I got into a really Zen place. My mind moved from one thing to the next like a dance.

Anyway, brainwaves can be measured by an EEG. Little scraggly lines that look like that chart.

We'll learn in BRILLIANCE II how to repeatedly have insights and not wait for some magical moment where God comes down from the mountain with commandments or Moses or some weird thing announcing changes in the world. We can repeat excellence in art, in creativity.

Insights are repeatable human behavior. I love that notion. CREATIVITY IS NOT MAGICAL, IT IS HUMAN.

CREATIVITY IS NOT MAGICAL, IT IS HUMAN.

A Library of the Mind

Mr. Bee handed out the reading lists for both semesters. He said, "If you can't take both semesters of BRILLIANCE, or have a friend not enrolled who'd like this info, here it is." I made a few comments along with Bee's.

I'll take BRILLIANCE II next semester. One of the assigned course books is The Art of Happiness by the Dalai Lama.

Happiness is an art. I love that. I also like school for the first time since I was a kid.

Mindsets by Dr. Carol Dweck (awesome, Stanford lady rocks!)

Virus of the Mind by Richard Brodie (the book is not all true, a joke you'll get after you read it.)

Brain Rules by John Medina (so informative!)

Your Brain at Work by David Rock (good stage references)

Flow by Dr. Flow (not going there again on that name)

The Mind Map Book by Tony and Barry Buzan (fun geniuses)

Art and Fear by David Bayles and Ted Orland (two artists who live it every day, freakin' awesome)

Second Semester BRILLIANCE Syllabus:

Lateral Thinking by Edward de Bono (hard reading, but great exercises)

Zing by Sam Harrison (a blast, love the book design)

The Art of Happiness by the Dalai Lama (life changer, thought provoker)

Caffeine for the Creative Mind by Stefan Mumaw and Wendy Lee Oldfield

<u>Jump Start</u> your Brain by Doug Hall

<u>A Whack on the Side of the Head</u> by Roger von Oech

<u>A Mind at a Time</u> by Mel Levine, M.D.

 The second semester will include more of both <u>Art and Fear</u> and <u>Mindsets</u>. Mr. Bee reserves the right to add or subtract books as he continues to learn.

The first semester establishes that we have brains and some control over what happens in them. We can use our brains for good or evil, status quo or creativity, to be a good witch or a bad witch. The second semester has exercises and a more hands-on approach to practical creative bettering of our minds. We are Brilliant.

Slim Jim

November 15 9:30 pm

Instead of a final exam in BRILLIANCE, our assignment is to find creative people and analyze what made them great artists, using material from the course.

I love Jim Carrey.   He makes me laugh.

Short Bios – Jim Carrey... ridiculous extravert, did comedy routines for classmates as a kid if he could keep his pie-hole shut during the day...at age 10, sent his resume to Carol Burnett, the most successful comedy show in America.

Homeless family, lived in a van...whole family worked as janitors during his childhood...moved to L.A. after dropping out of high school at 16...flopped as a stand-up, pestered Rodney Dangerfield into a job, failed in movies and again as stand-up... suffered through depression in the 1980's, kept working at his art... In 1990, at 28 got a break on *In Living Color*. *Ace Ventura Pet Detective* made him a star at 32.

As of today, he's a vegetarian. Jim was a straight "A" student until he dropped out of high school.

Committed growth mindset, failed and failed until he made it. He learned and believed in himself.

"If there had been Ritalin when I was a kid, I wouldn't be here now."

"I'm charming, but I dip into Prozac now and then," Jim Carrey

A great Jim Carrey growth mindset story: At one point, he was very successful in the comedy clubs just doing celebrity impressions and was coasting along, not growing as an artist. He didn't want to end up like Rich Little, a very successful impressionist, labeled as such, yet stuck in a rut doing the same act for forty years. Jim decided to dramatically change up his act until the audience booed him off. It was a wake-up call not to get too comfortable and to continue to grow. He actually courted boos. (perfect casting to portray creative genius, Andy Kaufman, in Man on the Moon.)

Wolfgang Amadeus Mozart – started composing at age five, but not good compositions. He started early, but not amazingly. He composed constantly and by 17 was a Salzburg court musician. He made very little money in his lifetime. He loved learning from others, borrowed from all the masters. His father was a concert teacher and composer and he'd sit next to his older sister when she took piano and played along. His father wrote down the songs he composed when he was five, and bragged to everyone how brilliant his son was, even before he did anything very well by adult standards.

Music in the home, art encouraged... the family business. His father cried when he did well, his sister played duets with him for the courts of Europe. Art was encouraged...failure never discussed...growth mindset...kept learning, from Bach and others he met. He admired and learned from everyone he could. Learning was his passion. Expanded from what he learned, innovated from the basics of others...

Small, thin, and scarred skin...dressed flamboyantly, spoke softly, worked long and hard...loved writing irreverently and with humor,...wrote a song, title translated, "Lick my ass, or kiss my ass." He challenged boundaries. He battled depression at times.

Twyla Tharp – A giant in American dance, she became a great choreographer, as great as any in our history. She worked at her parents store from the age of eight and was a bookworm when not working. She loved to read. When she started dance as a child she approached it like everything else, as a subject to be learned and explored. She experimented on the dance floor and combined classical, jazz, pop, and fused arrangements never seen before. Twyla Tharp put in 10,000 hours from the books, lessons, musical studies, and experimenting until she was considered a genius in her field.

<u>J's Lecture No.10</u>

How to be a Genius
The "Crap" Speech

Years ago, I attended a conference in which one of the sessions had a speaker named Paul Matthaeus from a motion graphics company called Digital Kitchen. The session was based on an article he wrote called Recognizing Creative Genius, so I thought I would attend.

In the article, Matthaeus talks about the attributes of creative geniuses:

Look at Problems From All Possible Angles

Make Their Thoughts Visible

Produce

Make Novel Combinations

Force Relationships

Think in Opposites

Think Metaphorically

Prepare Themselves for Chance

Paul did a great presentation and as he explained all the points, they made sense to me. There was, however, one concept that really stuck with me. It was number 3 on the list: Creative Geniuses produce.

It made common sense that the most successful people create a lot, but what hadn't occurred to me was that the best of the best and those often thought of as geniuses produce more "bad" works than less successful peers.

It was a light bulb moment for me. Wow, so the best guys produce more "crap" than other people. They explore more, take more risks, and "fail" more often. They PRACTICE, PRACTICE, PRACTICE. And because they practice more than most people, they learn more and have more results to choose from when they do have to compile examples of their work.

Tony Robbins suggests that "successful people" don't believe in "failure." They only look at things in terms of results. They always succeed in creating a result. It may not be the result they want, but that's ok because they will continue to make adjustments until they get the result they want.

So start today. Do more of that thing you want to be titled as. If you want to be a writer…write more. If you want to be a painter…paint more. If you want to be a dancer…dance more. If you…ok, I am sure you get the idea. The point is most of it may be "crap," but the more you do, the better you are going to get. Experiment and learn from your mistakes. Sometimes those happy accidents can lead to amazing and unexpected results.

Weird Dream

November 16 9:20 am

...glorious morning

Just woke up. This dream must've come from BRILLIANCE class... Yesterday we talked about accomplishment vs. activity and holy cow,... in my dream about this thing called "the module," it was a prize, a trophy, an award at this show like the Golden Globes only it was a Silver Rectangle.

All these men were pushing and shoving for it, playing mosh-pit wrestling to get at the module. Then female and male pop bands were on stage singing, scowling, and jamming for it, dressed like big-haired hookers playing atonal, awful noise.

Then all these pretty people were posing like models (Zoolander-style), all pouty lipped, vampy, vying for it. It was a shallow charade for this thing called the MODULE. It was a shiny, polished metal rectangle of silver pipes like a towel rack sculpture. All wanted to have a module. All were clueless. A dumb emcee hosted dumb people who filled the arena.

I think the module was fame or approval. It was an unhappy group of wannabes. No one was happy doing their vamp, or shoving, or showing off their breasts or hair. All just wanted the module, an empty box of shiny metal tubes. Shiny nothing, they worshipped shiny emptiness, "fame," an award for something they thought would bring them happiness.

Work Hard

November 16 10:03 am

"No one who rises before dawn three hundred sixty days a year fails to become rich." Chinese proverb from OUTLIERS.

What if I rise at 9:30 and work late?

Outliers: working hard is a big part of success. IQ tests give a head start, that's all.

Soon, others who work hard will catch up.

U.S. school year...180 days

Korea school year...220 days

Japan school year... 243 days

They aren't smarter or more talented, they work harder as kids.

Practice, Practice, Practice.

Cultures either lean towards rule-following or have a high ambiguity tolerance. Most U.S. schools tolerate very little ambiguity. We have lesson plans, grading, No child left behind...artists fail in traditional-thinking settings, far too constraining for the way creative thinkers process information and learn, and express back what's taught.

Creative thinking looks for possibilities and embraces ambiguity.

Logical thinking looks for the next step, the logical process, being right every step of the way.

Writing, pottery, painting, drawing, and composing all start with blank canvas, where there is no logic.

"Writing is easy: All you do is sit staring at a blank sheet of paper until drops of blood form on your forehead." ~ Gene Fowler

The always question is: What can we do to make a setting where we're more creative in our brain's invironment?

Creative thinking looks for possibilities and embraces ambiguity.

Logical thinking looks for the next step, the logical process, being right every step of the way.

Real Art

I'm experimenting with morning blogs, experimenting with time and awakeness and awareness.
 Lori, Mr. Bee and Mr. Fine touch my heart...these guys, they get it and are teaching us how to live as aliens in this world. Who are the aliens?

Mr. Bee bought the whole class copies of a book he calls his personal unveiling. The book is <u>Art and Fear</u>, written by working artists, David Bayles and Ted Orland.

He gave copies to Lori and Mr. Fine. It is source material for both of them. They all quote <u>Art and Fear</u> or paraphrase that book in their classes.

These artists, they're "grappling with the problem of making art in the real world. The observations they make are drawn from their real experience, and relate more closely to the needs of the artist than the interest of art viewers." <u>Art and Fear</u>

Their book says, "what it feels like to sit in your studio or classroom, at your wheel or keyboard, easel or camera, trying to do the work you do. It is about committing your future to your own hands, placing free will above predestination, choice above chance. It is about finding your own work."

On "Uncertainty" – "Materials are one of the few things we can control. The conditions are never perfect, humidity, noise...knowledge is incomplete on how or what you're creating, and few will understand what you're going through."

"Everything works out in the long run. I just wish it wasn't such a long run." J. Schuh, graphic artist and teacher.

"Art is human. To err is human; ergo, art is error." ~ <u>Art & Fear</u>

I laughed so hard I almost wet my pants when I read this.

It's time for sleep. Time to absorb the notion that others understand me. I am not alone as an artist. I have fellow travelers capable of articulating my life better than I can at this point.

Pots by the Pound

November 19 8:30 am

I awoke this morning and felt like a member of a community. I read a page of <u>Art and Fear</u> before breakfast then searched the internet for ideas.

"Only human beings, warts and all make art." <u>Art & Fear</u>

"It's important to know when a painting is finished, when to stop. You can ruin a piece by going past when it's done." Ruth Forbes Litwin

Mr. Fine got the idea of pots by the pound from Bayles and Orland.

No shortcuts to mastery.

No shortcuts to mastery.

"Art is human.
To err is
human; ergo,
art is error."
~ <u>Art & Fear</u>

<u>J's Lecture No.11</u>

Climbing the Ladder of Success

Becoming successful is hard. Rising in your field often feels like being the high-wire performer at a circus; people are secretly hoping you'll fall. This jealousy, along with the realization that success is a lot of hard work, leads to a fear of success. Let's face it, the higher you go up the ladder, the longer the fall.

The more successful you become, the more people will know what you have achieved. This means that many more people may become critical and jealous of your success. The risk involved in being creative means you will stumble and fall. That's part of being a risk taker – you fail sometimes. Your falls will be more public. Perception is reality. This includes your own perception of yourself. How do you handle it when you fall?

Years ago, I had a student in one of my classes who only showed up every once in awhile. He would show up to class late, sit down and sort of listen to my lectures and demonstrations. I have a coach mentality in my classes. If you don't work, you don't get much out of my classes. This student turned in his projects, but I could tell he had only put in just enough effort to meet the requirements of the assignments. Unfortunately, this is what most students do. In this kid though, I saw a spark in him that was different from the rest of the students. I saw potential in his work. That could have been the end of the story, but the next semester he signed up for another one of my classes.

When I saw him in my class again, I decided to see how strong his determination was and challenged him on both in-class and out-of-class assignments. I discovered he was smart and had the desire to succeed, but like most students, was dealing with various fears and trying to overcome bad habits. We talked a few times, and it took about half of that semester, but after achieving a few successes and discovering that he could succeed, a light bulb went on in his head and he got excited.

LADDER
TO
SUCCESS

LADDER
TO
SUCCESS

LADDER
TO
SUCCESS

Now imagine a ladder leading up against a wall. A normal person realizes that if you want to climb the ladder, you put your foot on the first rung and, holding on to the sides of the ladder for support, climb the ladder rung by rung. Not my student. Once he saw the potential, he wanted to get up the ladder as quickly as possible. So rather than wanting to go step-by-step up the ladder of mastery, he ran at the ladder and tried to grab a hold of the middle rungs. I think you can imagine the results.

If you were to try this with an actual ladder, I suspect there are two likely outcomes. The first one is as you try to grab the land on the rungs, your fingers slip or miss the sides, sending your body face-first into the ladder, hitting each rung as your body falls to the floor. The other probable outcome would be that you succeed in grabbing the sides and landing on the middle rungs where you aimed, but your momentum will bounce you off the wall as the ladder falls to one side or straight back. Either option involves pain. I recommend neither.

There are lessons to be learned by climbing each rung of the ladder. Don't try and cheat yourself out of the education, knowledge, and contacts you can acquire by climbing the ladder the way it was intended. Your dedication, discipline and ability to recognize and make the most of opportunities will determine how fast you climb the ladder to success in your area of interest.

"You ask why doesn't it come easily for me?"

The answer is, "because making art is hard!" ~ <u>Art & Fear</u>

Bee says: "As an artist you learn lessons over and over again...with a vengeance. In following the path of your heart, the chances are that your work will not be understandable to others...when wanting to be understood is a basic need...they say you're weird or crazy...but it comes from your heart, so are they right?   They're right that you're different from them."

"Do not let anything out of the studio you don't like. Please yourself."
~ Ruth Forbes Litwin

"Great art comes from the heart." ~ J Schuh

In class today, Mr. Bee acknowledged that not all artistic mediums have the same conditions for performance.

"Insulation periods are harder for performance artists, singers, music makers, actors in theatre, who reveal their souls and receive laughs, applause, and reviews. When you can, take some time before you reveal your work."

Dependence on an audience is a trap. Your new ideas might stretch the audience rather than be accepted with open arms. If they're uncomfortable with your stretching; they'll try to pass that baton to you.

Off to make pots...what a lot to think about with clay...shall I be daring today or make an ashtray?

Alec has a play reading I want to see tonight.

Long-neck

November 20 9:45 am

Alec's acting class performed monologues in front of the other actors and the art school students. Alec took a darker turn that worked for me. I didn't think that silly boy could get so serious. He's an actor. I forget that his art is using his emotions to make the audience feel. He's an artist using his body and soul to create a scene with no props or other actors...nicely done dude.

Inspired to be daring, I made a highly impractical giraffe chalice out of clay. It was too big to fit in the kiln, but Mr. Fine laughed so hard he shook. It was worth it to see him bounce, jiggle, and giggle.

The class loved my long-neck giraffe steins so much I made a smaller set that we could bake for drinking... Long Necks. They're so queer, but all the guys in the class love them. My friends clapped and laughed when I brought Long Neck to lunch. Alec only drinks beverages ending in "tini," but he gets the joke. Steven wants me to make four sets for Christmas presents. He'll buy them. Pay money for my art? It was a good adventurous art day.

...with a Cherry on Top!

November 21 8:50 am

It was the most fun I've had, being daring and risking with my long-necks. The fact that others enjoyed my experiment was the cherry on the sundae.

Mr. Bee quotes <u>Art and Fear</u>:

A good base from which to invent your own style is to know what's been done before.

Influence Exercise:

List six artists (in any field) that influence your work.

1. ____

2. ____

3. ____

4. ____

5. ____

6. ____

Approval –"The difference between acceptance and approval is subtle, but distinct. Acceptance means having your work counted as the real thing. Approval means having people like it, both audience related issues." ~ Art and Fear

Dangers of other-related issues...

"Courting acceptance puts much power in the hands of others...they're in a good vantage point of commenting on the finished product, but have little knowledge of the process. The audience comes later... the only pure communication is between you and your work." ~ Art and Fear

This issue of acceptance of result, the process, and arm-folded judgment are huge with Mr. Bee in his experience with clients.

"Between the first conversation and the finished project is an abyss we can see across, but never know exactly how we'll arrive." Mr. Bee And yet, the client will wish for you to bid time and money without really knowing the variables and what it will take for the thoughts to take physical shape.

Bee's initial response when asked for a price is usually, "It depends."
You're always guessing on your time, so ask lots of questions to narrow
the focus of what the client wants.

Yet when creating:
"For the artist the dilemma seems obvious: risk rejection by exploring
new worlds, or court acceptance by following well-explored paths."
~ <u>Art and Fear</u>

Mr. Fine adds, "In a practical sense, methods that work today usually
work tomorrow."

Practical Exercise:

List six methods that work for you now.

1. ____

2. ____

3. ____

4. ____

5. ____

6. ____

"For the artist the dilemma seems obvious: risk rejection by exploring new worlds, or court acceptance by following well-explored paths."
~ <u>Art & Fear</u>

Gobble-ette

November 22   7:53 am

I made my Dad a surprise for Thanksgiving...a Turkey Gobble-ette with a Dallas Cowboy star on it.

Holidays used to be salvation from school for me. With classes I love, I can't wait for school to start back up again. Happiness is in the doing, not the sitting around. I love making pottery now.   Reading and hearing thoughts of real artists in BRILLIANCE class gives me hope that I can be a professional artist.

Thanksgiving

November 25   11:20 pm

The highlight of Thanksgiving for my family is sitting with the cousins, uncles and Dad watching the Cowboys on TV. (I only watched the second quarter.) Alec came over and we went to his cast party Turkey-fest. My Dad beamed and bragged about his artist daughter as he drank Lone Star Beer from his turkey gobble-ette. I'm making five more for the other men in the family. ($25 a piece).

Alec, usually so supportive of me, quipped that he's going to petrify his feces and paint a Dallas Cowboy star on it for his family. They'll buy six. He may have a point in Dallas.

The Cowboy mugs are not risky art after the initial design...not even art at all except for the turkey-look, but it sells. I can see the dilemma right now. Produce to sell, or produce for the love of the piece. Can it be both?

Adoration

November 26 1:08 am

Alec's acting friends simply adore him, and he adores them. He had a romantic scene with Kathy, who knows he's gay, but wants him anyway, at least to be great friends. So when Kathy walked in late to the dinner party, Alec let out the girl-iest squeal/scream ever. We all laughed. Obviously, Alec adores Kathy too, but not in a sexual way. Then, I thought Bret was going to wet himself when Alec butched-up and asked some dumb football question after his falsetto scream. I love actors and singers. So open-hearted...we laughed a lot. Wine isn't my thing...I have a headache.

The Process

November 28 10:23 am

Lori, Fine, Bee and life are so "the process."

"The work you do tomorrow is shaped by the work you do today. Artist's work follows a continuum. The older stuff may be primitive, but it's the origins of your work today and tomorrow." ~ <u>Art and Fear</u>

The younger artists mess around with different mediums and tools and methods more so than older artists who have found elements they like and stick with them. Experimenting happens for older artists too, but less, with less reason to.

Lori wrote me back on my blog. She's really enjoying what I write, which is oddly satisfying that a real writer likes my work. She's still editing her movie.

Lori Keats, "The hard-won practical working habits we discover, and recurring forms that we can repeat, these habits that get us started, what gets us to write the first line, prepare the canvas, draw the body or face, embrace them."

I asked Mr. Fine about Lori's thought and he added,

"Working within the self-imposed style eases the mind on having to reinvent yourself with each new piece."

I'm sure I won't make my living as a sculptor or potter, but, the form, the feel, texture and dimension I'm learning with Professor Fine gives me tools and an artistic vocabulary for other work I'll do later on. Plus, it's really fun, and art, and I'm making a little money on the side using my Brilliant brain.

Maybe I'll animate 2-D or 3-D...be a commercial artist for print or design clothes with girly-girls...Right now I don't have to know where I'll be working or with who. I need to develop my brain, my skills, and be open to what the road offers. I'm in a good place, a learning place...a growth mindset with memes I choose.

I want to learn to create on my stage, on command, when I want to, and not wait for magic or the special mood to arise.

Lori Keats, "The hard-won practical working habits we discover, and recurring forms that we can repeat, these habits that get us started, what gets us to write the first line, prepare the canvas, draw the body or face, embrace them."

Inspiration Exercise:

List four inspirations for getting started.

1. _______________________________________

2. _______________________________________

3. _______________________________________

4. _______________________________________

Inspiration Exercise:

List four inspirations that keep you working.

1. _______________________________________

2. _______________________________________

3. _______________________________________

4. _______________________________________

Fail to Succeed

Marina Semyonova was one of the greatest ballerinas of all time. Born in Czarist Russia, her teens were spent during the Lenin/Stalin revolution. Art was even more challenging in those harsh times. She became a symbol of hard work, great form, and an ambassador of artistic interpretation to the world. Considered the greatest ballet teacher of all time, she taught dance well into her 90's.

Marina chose her students in a completely growth mindset manner.

Those youngsters who were great already she was less interested in than those who worked hard and dared to make mistakes.

Eva is back with us after learning
the new difficult routine.

Ballerina drawing, rubbing her sore knee or falling down trying something new.

She knew that growth comes from trying the harder tasks rather than mastering easier tricks or jumps.

The girls who fell and got up to try again were her prized pupils and ultimately best dancers.

The gist is, work hard, fail, get up, and work hard, fail and one day I'll succeed. I get it. It also helps to find the medium where I have talent, passion and love for the art so I love even the failed pieces.

Tom Hanks

November 29 8:23 am

When I was really young, my parents told me that I could succeed at anything I put my mind to. That gradually changed to, "we thought you were smart," which changed to, "some kids are more gifted," which then changed to, "not everyone can be good in school," to finally, "please just graduate." They often told me I was wasting my time drawing instead of doing homework. They were never abusive, just unaware of how I experience the world.

Tom Hanks went to twelve schools in twelve years. He had a "fractured childhood" as he calls it, with no abuse, just confusing parental messages. I can relate.

Tom took no acting classes, but was drawn to theatre and film as his life's work because of his background. Being the new kid time after time, he adapted to roles and played the parts he perceived would work for him in each environment.

His brain was wired by his life to be an actor.

Failing to get a part in a junior college play, he went to the community theatre and started there with little success, but he loved it.

Love and commitment with hard work allowed Tom Hanks to win

Oscars, play great parts, and have an adventurous life on screen.

"I've made over 20 movies and 5 of them are good."

"In this business, careers are based on longevity."

"My work is more fun than fun, but best of all, it's still very scary…like athletes that retire, they'll tell you the moment when the ball comes your way, there is no moment like that in their lives…with acting, I can do it until I'm old…If I didn't have the chance to do what I do, I would miss more than anything, that feeling, unlike anything else in the world." Tom Hanks

House of Mouse

November 30 7:50 pm

Bee showed us a video about the man who drew Mickey Mouse. Walt Disney was Mickey's voice, while Ub Iwerks drew Mickey. What a name?! Ub Iwerks is not a misprint. Check out the 110 minute video if you can ever find it, The Hand Behind The Mouse. It was on YouTube, then got pulled.

Ub was a skilled artist who began with simple hand drawings and inking in cels. As he grew with the industry, he pioneered technology used by Disney into the 1970's. He innovated his entire career, to the benefit of anyone who ever loved cartoons.

The beginnings of animation, and the middles too, were influenced by his drawings, but even more so by his engineering. The classic, 101 Dalmatians, wouldn't have happened without Iwerks and Xerox Corporation collaborating on higher-speed coloring of cels. His Academy Award was for technology later in his career, even though he drew Mickey Mouse. What a life he had! See that documentary. It's AWESOME and INSPIRING!!!

Equinox

December 1 9:23 am

I'm getting sad that this semester is almost over. With the time change and planet tilt this time of year, the days are shorter, the nights longer. It's getting colder. The good news, I'm getting more hours during the holidays at Banana Republic. I can use the money, but am clear that retail sales are not my path long-term. They do have some cool clothes though, and I get a discount.

I made 89 pounds and got pretty good at throwing pots in the process. I love pottery, but it's not my bliss. Next semester, I'll take BRILLIANCE II, and English 102, with the same teacher and blog assignment.

What's easier than writing my thoughts for an A, and getting better at writing too? I'm taking animation with Mr. Bee and will apprentice for him, for maybe some pay??? We haven't worked out the details, yet.

I like school this year for the first time since second grade. I feel like I belong. I get to choose what I want to study, more so than ever. Control over my life, focus on goals, having time fly by in flow,... feeling like my skills are improving. I feel like an adult in control of parts of my life. Knowing about Flow, the flow guy, Mr. Bee, ...the whole, long, reading list, I'm excited about my future as an artist more now than ever.

Art for Food

December 2 11:12 pm

Today at Banana, I got to re-work a window display...It was so fun I can't believe it! Art in retail??? I won't shut that door, who knows? Dressing models with clothes in window displays uses color, design, space...I was really happy at work and made money...

Have Artist Brain, Will Work for Food and Clothes

HAVE ARTIST BRAIN
WILL WORK FOR FOOD

I've been sleeping and eating better and it shows up in my attitude. I haven't been depressed since Steven dumped me. We never dated, but it felt like rejection in my mind. Attitude and Sleep...now there's a book every artist, maybe every person could connect with.

Closet Artists

December 4 11:05 pm

Less time to read with a mostly full work schedule and my classes. I miss the symphony of artistic voices from school, but do love the extra money. Dad's been totally off my back since the Gobble-ettes and me making more money at Banana and in pottery sales.

Mom and Dad came by the mall to look at my displays. Mom got teary-eyed. Dad bought a shirt and hugged me at my job. He mumbled something about liking the display. Mom commented on the compositions and relationship of space. Does she take me seriously? Did she take art classes? I was shocked about what she knew. Is Mom a closet artist? They were proud of me. Stupid to care about that, but I guess I still want their approval.

Fixed Thinking

December 6 8:46 pm

Bee gave a lecture today, almost apologetic in tone. This is my reflective summary:

He said stuff like, "I apologize if it seemed that I bashed fixed thinking...it's just not creative thinking, but not worse kind of thinking. We teach fixed thinking and overuse it, but it is certainly important to artists, too. Fixed thinking has vital uses. Engineers, medical techniques, pharmacy procedures, brain surgery, anything with lasers, automotive, plumbing...where you need measurable standards, we need left-brain process.

The main negative about fixed thinking is how it bullies growth thinking. When trying to measure the value of artists, it inevitably feels like fixed thinkers bully growth thinking processes. Measure yourself, rate yourself, quantify why you should exist?!

Arts programs get cut first in education, because it's so hard to value what numbers can't measure.

What's the value of drawing, acting, singing, composing? Numbers on art? ...that's what's so maddening.

Knowledge of science can help art...mixing paints using 10% umber, or five per cent red, detailing proportions and scale in drawing, composing songs using fourth and sixteenth notes, rests, and rhythms... fixed and measurable are useful, just not better than growth thinking.

Failing is required in growth thinking, and failure is feared in fixed thinking. Neither is better, just different and important at different times.

Knowing what the Eiffel Tower looks like, what the Bolshoy ballet is, or having an appreciation for architecture in Prague...all can inspire more creativity in your store window, your animation, or your being human-ness. Being an artist is no excuse for not learning about the many interesting things in the world.

"All science touches on art, and all art has a scientific side. The worst scientist is he who is not an artist. The worst artist is he who is not a scientist." ~ Armand Trousseau

Bee makes sure we don't turn into artistic bullies or lazy people. Just because creative thinking is brilliant doesn't mean other forms of brilliance don't exist.

It's fixed thinking to imagine yours is the only right way of thriving, being, or finding success.

“All science touches on art, and all art has a scientific side. The worst scientist is he who is not an artist. The worst artist is he who is not a scientist.”
~ Armand Trousseau

Fixed Thinking Exercise:

List five careers where fixed thinking can be useful.

1. ____

2. ____

3. ____

4. ____

5. ____

So Lenny, a white rapper who's actually really good, stood up, raised his fist and yelled, "Right on Mr. Bee. Some of us read the books, others write them. I'm writing them."

Mr. Bee laughed and called bullshit. "Read and explore the history of your art. Listen to albums, go to galleries…inspiration isn't in a vacuum. Borrow the tools of those before you. Do you really need to invent fire, the wheel, or a piano?"

Unknown Exercise:

List five areas you know nothing about.

1. _______________________________

2. _______________________________

3. _______________________________

4. _______________________________

5. _______________________________

Unknown Exercise II:

Imagine and make up things you might gain by exploring the above list. (No wrong answers here.)

1. _______________________________

2. _______________________________

3. _______________________________

4. _______________________________

5. _______________________________

Schtick

December 9 8:28 am

This is the last week of class this semester, and I'm so busy, scheduled for fifty-five hours at the mall on top of school. I got Alec a part-time, three-week gig at Banana. That boy can sell and flirt. He's so charming and ballsy. What he says to girls and grown women would make Hugh Hefner blush. Sassy...he's just a sassy man who makes selling a performance art. I gotta think bigger...Creative thinking is way more than classroom theory.

I'm pretty sure he'd get fired for some of his dialogue, but it sure works for Christmas shoppers when our supervisors are too busy to monitor his comedic stylings, or as Ginger calls it, his "schtick."

Memes

December 10 8:19 am

Memes are the building blocks of culture.

Memes support a culture's survival, reproduce values, and steer the minds of the culture's inhabitants.

Bee's reviewing for BRILLIANCE II, and for those whom he never sees again. Did I just write the word "whom"? Now that's funny for an art major!!!! Whom do I think I am?

Gingo gave me a copy of the <u>Four Agreements</u>, by Don Miguel Ruiz. She ranted that we're all brainwashed. Agreed upon values or memes are not sufficiently challenged. I don't have time to debate or read her book. I'm in school and working at the mall. She calls me a sell-out. I call her Gingo. Thanks for caring, Gingo, and for questioning. I'll question more when I have time. Gingo dropped out of school this semester. I told her I'd read the book if she'd take BRILLIANCE.

Culture changes through questioning.

Culture changes
through
questioning
and memes are
the building
blocks of culture.

We don't have to rant to question. The more we know, the more we know how to question more effectively and what resembles a new paradigm worth following. It's one thing to question, another to be open to an answer we might not be comfortable with. Questioning and rebelling aren't the same thing.

Down and Dirty

December 11 8:55 am

Bee got down and dirty today.

Hard-wired biological responses are called "instincts." They took millions of years to evolve. They exist for survival of the species, survival of the DNA. As culture has evolved, some instincts are poorly adapted to modern life, yet exist nonetheless.

Memes are created by minds, mutated by minds, or denied entry by minds.

Memes are created by minds, mutated by minds, or denied entry by minds.

Rebelling against memes still engages the meme.

Since all thoughts are human-made, there is no truth with a capital "T".

That's what I'm trying to tell Ginger, that she's still playing with the same meme by fighting against it, rather than removing it from her stage. Interview the thought, then throw the bum out if he's disturbing your performance, rehearsal, or creative space in any way. Be in control of your stage.

Mr. Bee talked the whole class about memes again. How we see ourselves, how we see the world, is only as real as we imagine it to be, what memes we believe in. We create our reality by what we think and who we attract onto our stage.

When you fight against something, you give it importance. Remove it, or ignore it and it wilts from lack of attention.

Meme Deletion Exercise:

Name four memes you'd like to explore removing from your consciousness. (Again, no wrong answers here).

1. ____

2. ____

3. ____

4. ____

Since all thoughts are human-made, there is no truth with a capital "T".

Meme Addition Exercise:

Name five memes you'd like to explore adding to your consciousness. (No wrong answers.)

1. ____

2. ____

3. ____

4. ____

5. ____

Ritualistic

December 12 9:01 am

Today was about "Patience." Most great artists don't receive acclaim while alive. The adoration they'd like to have for their ground-breaking contributions take time, since by definition, "ground-breaking is new to the medium and takes time for the world to catch on." ~ <u>Art and Fear</u>

The word posthumous means after we die. "Post-humorous" means its funny later. Comedy is hard.

We talked in pottery today more than at any time.

Mr. Fine said "We'd best enjoy the process, because the rewards are in the process, or it's likely not worth doing."

Bee came into our class to see what Mr. Fine's students had done. He was beautifully kind to us all and bought a few pieces. Fine asked Bee to say a few words.

"Discipline gets you to the typewriter or easel. Once you have good habits or have found a medium or style you like, keep doing it unless pain or boredom overtakes you."

Someone asked Bee how he does his art.

Bee answered, "My rituals are mine alone, but an apple slice, hard boiled egg, coffee and two donuts is my norm. An early morning swim four days a week, a power smoothie instead of lunch. I walk with my wife most evenings and give her lots of hugs. She hugs back, so I get lots, too. Find whatever habits or rituals get you and keep you going. What works, works."

Ritual Exercise:

Name six rituals that are working for you.

1. ____

2. ____

3. ____

4. ____

5. ____

6. ____

Rituals Not Working Exercise:

List three habits or rituals that are not working for you.

1. ____

2. ____

3. ____

"Discipline gets you to the typewriter or easel. Once you have good habits or have found a medium or style you like, keep doing it unless pain or boredom overtakes you."

Bloggers note:

My mental stage, my PFC, is still developing...the Pre-frontal cortex
doesn't fully develop until my late 20's. That's a relief,...I'll be better at
organizing my life and thoughts as I get older.

Steven made a funny, but good argument...if Ginger wants to do drugs
in her 30's, when she can make good decisions with a fully developed
brain, go for it. Until her brain is developed fully, which it won't be if
she does drugs, she shouldn't make that decision.

Julie Taymor

December 13 8:03 am

Alec wants to see *Spiderman"* on Broadway. In the musical, they fly
across the auditorium. He made me watch "60 Minutes" Sunday night
about the making of *Spiderman, the Musical.* Bono and The Edge from
U2 are doing the music and the lady who did Lion King, Julie Taymor
is the director. Julie sculpted the masks, painted them, helped with
music, supervised the choreography, designed the sets, choreographed
the flying on four wires for multiple actors, worked with the engineers...
and was scared the whole time. She inspires me so much.

Julie said, "I love it when people say, what a lousy idea. I hate the
comfort zone. I don't think anything can be done that's creative
without danger and risk...if you don't fear, then you aren't taking a
chance."

She goes on to say, "What I do have is a team of collaborators,
empowered and passionate, that mitigates the fear."

I want to be her. I want a creative mental stage as big as hers is to cross
mediums. I know I'm not fully formed in my brain, but the more I
work those neural paths, the more paths I have to combine mediums.

What can I do to develop myself?   Brilliance is a good start.
BRILLIANCE II will help. Diet, exercise, sleep, classes, challenges. I'm
so fired up!!!!!!!!!

I want a life where I can grow and challenge and feel like I make a difference, where I touch people in a good way.

Humans from 14 to 24 years of age need 9.5 hours of sleep...that number drops to 7.5 to 8 as we mature. Teenagers' circadian rhythms make them want to stay up later, and school starts so damn early That's an unnatural state of being. Lower test scores in early morning classes reflect sleep needs un-met.

Gems

December 14 9:14 am

"The personal nature of art is unique in that a realtor or accountant doesn't view their inner being as intimately involved as you do with your art. The direct correspondence between your very soul and what you show the world makes for a more sensitive interaction with the outside world." ~ <u>Art & Fear</u>

Lori Keats said, "Artists are affected more by the outside world. We must protect ourselves from overly critical people. Of course, not all of our work deserves praising either."

Mr. Bee gives us gems that combine things we've learned this semester. This is one of my favorites.

"Good art challenges the audience and presents a danger to their thoughts. Any fixed thinking parts of the world others have created in their minds are targets for art. The more effective the art, the more emotional reactions occur, usually negative. Then they search for who's to blame for this outrage."

"If you're part of the new, you threaten the old."

This sums up the first semester:

I can create a mind in control of my thoughts, a stage where I can combine elements, and I can be an artist who lives a life filled with days of flow and passion for what I do.

When I get depressed, I nap, move, or eat something healthy. I can think positive or negative thoughts. I'm in charge of me and I'm brilliant when I take charge of my mind.

Creatives, agents of change, go through lots of changes, so get used to it.

Why I love BRILLIANCE..............

From Outliers...there are no naturals in any field who didn't work towards mastery, no musicians, artists, painters...all had talent and worked to get into good schools or find good teachers where their work ethic brought them to mastery.

"I am brilliant. I am an artist. I think differently, and I will change the world."

Mary

Creatives, agents of change, go through lots of changes, so get used to it.